ENDORSEMENTS

From his supernatural conversion on the roadside through his immediate miraculous deliverance from alcohol abuse, Tom will capture your heart. His amazing testimony of how supernatural peace is available to all those that seek God. His gifted teaching on how forgiveness can bring transformation to any family in turmoil will not only grab your attention, it will grab your heart as well. It's a must read.

—Dr. Thomas J. McCoy
(Tom's pastor and friend for nearly 20 years)

I have heard some of the stories of Tom's life situations, but I grew to respect and appreciate his life and friendship even more after seeing his "heart" in writing. I saw the love he had for his family and his family for him and I know he loves Jesus. I had never heard him talk about forgiveness nor have I heard it explained the way Tom explains it between these covers. That description of forgiveness had a tremendous effect on my life and my attitude toward others. All of us, at some point in our life, will need to ask forgiveness for our sinful nature. We all fall short of God's mercy and do not deserve His Grace. I pray the words in this book will speak to you as they have spoken to me. Especially the way Tom describes Forgiveness. Saying, "I'm sorry" is easy. Forgiveness, not so much. True forgiveness, the way Tom describes it, well don't miss it.

—James Alderson
Friend - Founder ONSITE Pros, Inc.

For years, Tom Toner has been committed to the primary care of people's spiritual health in the workplace. His "down to earth" bedside manner never feels churchy or judgmental. You will find Tom's spiritual revelations in his book resonate with the reader through his own very personal struggles and humble transparency. "Heart at Work" is his prescription for a healthy walk with the Lord in today's world.

—Celeste LaReau
Founder, Tennessee
Christian Chamber of Commerce

When a family member in serious condition was hospitalized for 52 days, Tom stepped into my life. He showed up every day at a time when my husband and I felt shattered with no close family living near us. Tom epitomized a heart at work; his heart worked overtime for us.

—Ginger Hoogesteger - Friend

Tom is currently serving our company as Our Company Chaplain/Pastor. He has taken his 25 years as a pastor and put it in a book for everyone to read. Tom has demonstrated to our Servant Leaders that his heart is at work from the inside out. He cares for the employees as a father, or a brother, would care for someone they love. This book is the culmination of just some of his life experiences and personal involvement in the lives of the people He has served. It is a must read for working people and leaders that desire to influence others.

—Joe Rodgers
President, Civil Constructors
Nashville, TN

Hearts at Work

*How to Powerfully Practice,
Passionately Pursue, and
Purposely Persuade by Your Faith*

TOM TONER - THE PEOPLES CHAPLAIN
AUTHOR/SPEAKER/COACH

Primary Editor - Marguerite Bonnett
Associate Editors – Ginger Hoogesteger
Laurie Kamunen
Cover Design – Heidi Caperton
Audio Book Engineer – Thomas D. Toner
Interior Design – Allison Toner Hoog

ISBN:
Paperback: 978-1-64746-780-7
Hardback: 978-1-64746-781-4
Ebook: 978-1-64746-782-1

Library of Congress Control Number: 2021908173

"Trust in the Lord with all your heart,
And lean not on your own understanding;
In all your ways acknowledge Him,
And He shall direct your paths".
Proverbs 3:5-6 (NKJV)

"And whatever you do, do it heartily,
as to the Lord and not to men,
knowing that from the Lord you will
receive the reward of the inheritance;
for you serve the Lord Christ."
Colossians 3:24-25 (NKJV)

Dedication

First, I give all the glory to God for the content of this book. He sharpened me along the way and educated me more times than I would like to admit. God reminded me that He is in charge and that I'm on earth to serve Him and every person He brings my way.

To my wife, Janice Toner, the love of my life who believed in my passionate desire to write this book. She has been by my side for over 41 years through great times and not-so-great times. Without her support and encouragement, this book would not exist. I am grateful to God for bringing her into my life.

To my three children April, Allison, and Thomas, I thank you for all the times we experienced growing up. This book helped me reflect on just how fast life goes by as well as the important impact of a mother and a father. I am so proud of the people you have become. I love you.

To my friend and colleague, Jerry Weaver, who went to be with our Lord this year, our hearts laughed together.

Thank You Corporate Chaplains of America for 15 great years of helping develop my character and understanding of how God can be exalted in the workplace. What I learned through CCA has continued to impact those in and out of the workplace. Thank you, CCA.

To the experts in the publishing world of Throne Publishing, Jeremy Brown, and the crew along with Author Academy Elite, I thank you for holding my hand through the process.

Thank you to my brothers and sisters in Christ that encouraged me to share my experiences with others. When you encouraged me, my confidence soared.

To my Tampa, Florida cousin Carol and her husband Gary for planting the seed to get the publishing rolling. I'm grateful for the impact you had on my work.

CONTENTS

PART THREE

INTRODUCTION

The Heart – A vital organ that lasts well over eighty years if we are blessed. The heart is constantly beating at a healthy average of about eighty beats a minute for a long time, extraordinary! When the heart stops, the blood ceases to flow throughout our bodies, all the vital organs die, we die! Or so, I thought! What a way to start a book. Death as its beginning yet this is a book about life.

My heart began beating in March of 1958 in New York City. I am the son of a father who spent over 35 years of his life as an insurance investigator for what is now called Equifax. I am the oldest of 5 siblings to a mother who loved being a mother. As with all kids, the influence of my parents and teachers developed in me a core of ideas, behaviors, and principles. What I believed to be true about life followed me into a career with the U.S. Air Force, a long-lasting marriage with three angelic children. Only kidding about the angelic children, they were too much like their father.

I was a high school athlete with an Irish Catholic heritage and an attractive sense of humor. A skinny, prejudiced city kid, who knew nothing about the world outside of the rushing fire hydrant on a hot summer day and constant stickball games in the concrete jungle. In fact, I had no idea a person could own a cow. The only cows I knew were the boring cows I saw at the Bronx Zoo as we walked past them to get to the monkeys. I had plenty to learn.

This book is about real life, from The Bronx to Eternity. You may relate to many of the things you read – life experiences transcend culture. Leaving the shelter of mom and dad and joining the Air Force where I met people from all over the world, has given me a deep appreciation for life. The seasons of getting married and raising children while developing a career sped up the maturation process.

Life's journey begins and ends with decisions that follow us forever, some good and some bad. As we learn from these decisions, we become molded by them and that determines what we pass on for generations to come.

A few years back, I concluded that whatever I experienced so far in life, I had to share with other people. What value would I add to others if I kept these lessons to myself? Maybe someone else can learn and grow from my experiences. I've learned that life has purpose. The purpose may be known, but often, it just passes. Our stories are unique and, in many ways, surprisingly similar. The internal workings of the heart and mind are remarkable. When the heart and mind work together, they produce life changing results that grow us, influence others, and leave a legacy.

The intricacies of the physical body are nothing less than spectacular. Not one vital organ can function on its own. We all have the same set-up. Six major systems that need to work properly: 1. Circulatory 2. Respiratory 3. Digestive 4. Nervous 5. Muscular 6. Skeletal. Amid all these systems, the heart must continuously pump blood throughout. I know what you're thinking, the Tin Man in the Wizard of Oz did not have a heart. That is another story and by the way he did get one later.

I propose to you my friends, that not only do we need the physical heart to keep our body going. We also need a spiritual heart to understand, experience, interact, teach, and learn who our Creator is and what His intended purpose is for all of us. His name is God and ours is mankind. What good is keeping the heart alive if we do not practice its spiritual significance? We would be more like robots than unique, expressive, purposeful people who can exercise choices for the good of our fellowman. Imagine your journey from the spiritual heart. This book talks about my journey.

My story chronicles real life transformation from the inside out. Realizing that each of us has a spiritual aspect to our lives, our hearts are at work more than just in the physical sense. Our hearts are broken, softened, hardened, and shared many times during our life journey. We give it away – many times without a second thought. Our ideas are tied to the heart and our emotions show themselves when we least expect it. We often break the hearts of the ones we love without intention.

The heart is at work from childhood until the day when it beats no more.

The compelling choice to change my journey was a supernatural event for me - and maybe it has been for you. Or maybe there still a change in you that needs recognition and development. The God of my youth was far away and impersonal, but that changed dramatically in my early thirties. My greatest hope is that my story inspires you to take your own journey deep into your Spiritual Heart, and then allow your heart to guide you as a Christian leader.

Thank you for taking a minute to read this introduction. All I ask is that while you are reading this book, think practically, understanding that we have no idea what God can do through us, or in us, unless we ask Him!

May God richly bless you as you read this book.

PART ONE
MOMENTS OF FAITH

CHAPTER ONE
ATTACK OF THE HEART

I had to pull over to gather my thoughts. It took a minute, but that moment was not the time to keep driving. Have you ever noticed just how fast life changes? It happens every day; someone's life changes in a moment. Rich people, poor people, people who are in great physical condition, and folks who are in poor health. Our finances, our family, our home life can change with just one tragedy. On the other hand, life can have great changes, just as fast. We can get a perfect new job; buy the dream house we always wanted or get a clean bill of health from our family doctor after a long illness. The chapter you are about to read is real. Life changed instantly for me and this is how it happened.

San Antonio, Texas, home of the Riverwalk and the Alamo. I had a wife who loved me, three beautiful children and an exciting career teaching in the world's finest Air Force. Socially, I was adapting well to the cowboy lifestyle, even though I grew up in the Bronx. Notice "I" was adapting well. We will get into that later.

The Air Force assigned us to various bases throughout the ten years prior to our arrival in Texas and our family was growing with each move. Our girls were just two years apart and our son was about 9 months old when I landed my dream job as an Air Force Recruiter Instructor in San Antonio, Texas. There were about fifteen people in the nation who could say they were teaching Air Force sergeants to recruit for the Force. Teaching at the national level was extremely rewarding for a young staff sergeant. My ego was being fed daily.

My marriage seemed to be going well. Janice, my wife of ten years, was caring for our girls and our newborn son. Always finding time to cook up fabulous meals after work and keeping the house in order. I would say that our relationship was solid. The biggest challenge for Janice and me were our personality differences. I was a loudmouth, boisterous, life of the party, city boy. She was an introverted, quiet, country girl, mother, and wife that fit perfectly into my life. There were small arguments if I did not get my way, but they did not last long. I looked forward to a good career with an ideal situation at home.

My work as a teacher fit like a glove. I had a class of about twenty-five students every seven weeks or so. I would teach them how to recruit from the civilian world into the Air Force way of life. It was a thorough six-week intensive course on the strategies of changing from a civilian to an Airman.

My wife Janice served honorably in the Air Force for four years. We met at our first base in 1978, got married in 1980 and were stationed in England for the first three years of our marriage. We both decided that Janice would finish up her commitment in uniform and we would begin a family. That was a decision that we never regretted.

Damage Control

My wife and I were having arguments more and more often. I did not think much of the impact of our friction until one Friday night, on the way home from work. I stopped at the gas station to get a sixteen-ounce Budweiser for the fifteen-minute journey home. I normally stopped for a beer almost every Friday night. But this one Friday was different.

I got my beer and started driving home. I knew there would be an argument waiting in the living room, because 1) I had a beer and 2) I was going to tell Janice I wanted to go on a trail ride for the weekend with a few of my cowboy friends. By the way, I had become a pseudo cowboy since I moved from New York to Texas. I had all the proper attire such as boots, Stetson hat, jeans, and BIG belt buckles. I had absolutely no idea what I was doing trying to fit in.

Be careful whenever you start a story with "I got my beer."

Everyone has a story of how their lives were affected growing up with their family. My story was dominated by alcohol abuse. Your story may be different, but the effect will remain.

As a young child, I spent many hours in neighborhood bars with both of my parents. I had been drinking alcohol most of my life - from the beginning of my teenage years. Alcohol was part of growing up. You see the irony here, *growing up and alcohol?* Being surrounded by the abuse, you tend to repeat the abuse. Drinking was a part of my life and I carried it into my relationship with my family. My heart was not in the right place. Personal insecurities showed their ugly head in my actions, and alcohol was my coping mechanism. Drinking was just one action that kept me on a road of selfish ambition. I know that now, but I did not recognize the struggle when I thought everything was going well.

Hidden Heavy Heart

I was running from something, but I had no idea where I was going. Did you ever do that? Run from something that is going on internally, but not realize what the struggle or the pain associated with the action was all about? Life seemed smooth most of the time. I had a woman who loved me, kids that greeted me at the door after work, and a job that put me in the limelight on a national scale. What else can you ask for?

As I drove home, my mind took me back to the days of watching my parents struggle with alcohol. Alcoholism destroyed my father, and my mother hid the pain she suffered by the actions of my father - before they divorced. The more I thought about what happened when I was young, the more emotional I was becoming. My heart seemed to melt; thoughts overwhelmed me so much I had to pull over on the side of the road. My mind was racing. I was preparing to go home and fight with my wife because I wanted to go out and party with friends for the weekend. But a part of me did not want to argue anymore. I was tired of the drama.

Something Strange Was Happening

As I sat in my car by the side of the road, I began to weep uncontrollably. This was real and I had no idea why. I could not control my tears. I cried out to God, who I did not know, I asked Him to take the desire for alcohol away and help me stop arguing with my wife as I sat there with a sixteen-ounce

Budweiser, crying like a baby but not knowing why. Physically I was drained, but mentally I was broken.

The only way I can describe this moment is that God had me where He wanted me, admitting that my life was on a road to destruction. I felt as though I was losing my wife and family based on my self-absorbed behavior. I began to realize what Tom's so-called success was all about.

Can I Talk About God? No Religion in This House

The word "I" is used often because life was about me back then, unintentionally disregarding my family. I had some idea that God cared for my family. I certainly was not a religious guy. God was not even in the picture. I was agnostic, at best. Agnostic is just another way to say, "You believe what you believe. I don't care." As a teenager, I would drink with the priest in the park across from the Catholic school I attended. My relationship with God was limited to what I learned from those who were my teachers. I loved my priests in high school. They weren't bad people, but they rarely talked about Jesus or even what they believed personally.

Broken Heart Needs Repair

Back in my car on the side of the road after what seemed like a good hour, I stopped crying and a peace overwhelmed my heart. This peace was indescribable. I looked around as if I was experiencing a dream. I poured out my sixteen-ounce Budweiser and remained still for another ten minutes. I was never treated for drug or alcohol abuse. Never even thought about entering an Alcoholics Anonymous program. Something powerful was happening that could only be described as a miracle. The only miracle I knew was "Miracle on 34th Street", the classic Christmas movie.

The source of this miracle had no natural explanation, it was supernatural. All I did was ask God to help me, and He changed my heart in that moment. Now what? Something needed to happen, but I did not know even the next heartbeat.

What I did know was that I asked God, who I had no personal relationship with, to help me with my actions and my relationship. A sudden, overwhelming, peace came over me shortly after I asked for His help. I cannot even remember exactly what I did when I got home. I do know, I did not go on the trail ride that weekend. I was simply different. My attitude, my mindset, and my actions changed. Overall, my perspective about life began to change. I would learn quickly what a heart change looked like for me and my family. Any change takes time to adapt and practice. God had taken me and began a good work in me that continues to this day.

No Denominations in Sight

Church. Yes, that's right, church. That must be the next step I thought. There were a bunch of churches in San Antonio. I visited the closest one to my house. I had no idea about denominations because I was raised in a Catholic church. I stopped by a church called Village Parkway Baptist Church. I knew I should go and speak with the Pastor, so I did just that. He would be the one to help me figure out what happened on the road. So, here I go to tell the story of my life change to a Pastor I didn't even know.

After I explained the unexplainable the best I could, the Pastor asked me if I knew Jesus. Of course, I knew Jesus. He was the one on the cross. He died, was buried, and rose again. I knew the Act of Contrition and the stations of the cross, as any good Catholic altar boy should.

Same Jesus, Different Looking Cross

Here is what the pastor told me: Jesus is no longer on the cross. He ascended into heaven and sits at the right hand of the Father. He came to earth just to die for me so that I could live for Him and with Him forever. He also told me that when Jesus ascended to heaven, He sent His Holy Spirit to help us with this life. Aha! That was what happened to me in the car. God's Spirit overwhelmed me and convicted me to change my perspective. That explained it for me, and I got excited about the good news (gospel). I began a closer walk with God from that point on. That was 1988. A lot has happened since then, but this moment was real, and no one could ever convince me of anything different.

Understanding Who is First?

What comes first in our life is an important part of who we are. *Who* comes first is probably a better question to ask. It was clear to me that the Air Force had been a priority for me. I spent twenty years dedicated to serving our country. They told me I was the best. I earned numerous plaques that I proudly displayed on the walls of my recruiting office. The awards showed just how dedicated I was to the mission. After my encounter on the road, I was convinced that the government generally does not care one bit about my family or me. If you serve them, you will be in good standing. I clearly remember a popular saying, "If the Air Force wanted you to have a family, they would have issued you one."

If I had a nickel for every time I heard about someone getting divorced because they worked sixty to seventy hours a week for years, I would be rich. Priorities often become important when you mess them up. I sure did!

Do not get me wrong. I loved what I did for a living. I had no regrets about joining the Air Force, not one! I put my job first, and my wife and children after me. Maybe some of you can relate to having your priorities out of order. Unfortunately, this is a common practice for us human beings. I'm convinced that my marriage would have ended in divorce if God's transformation in me had not taken place. The writing was on the wall. I had to discover the importance of what is important.

I began to understand that God created me first for Him, then gave me a family to nurture, then a job to develop skills and make an income to support my family. In that order, according to His plan, not mine. Life was not about only me anymore. I had plenty to learn about His plans.

My spiritual perspective started to become clearer. I began a disciplined Bible study in the book of John. I needed to learn more about the life and works of Jesus. One verse I had memorized from the beginning was in the Book of Proverbs, the third Chapter, Verse 5-6. (NKJV) "Trust in the Lord with all your heart and lean not on your own understanding; in all your ways acknowledge Him, And He shall direct your path."

I learned that if we have our priorities any other way, they are misaligned with the direction God has set for you and me. We may not know it until we leave Him out long enough to experience our own futility. Pride will show up on our front door with a destroying attitude. The Bible reads in Proverbs 11:2 (NLT) "Pride leads to disgrace, but with humility comes wisdom."

Personal Priorities with Perseverance

I totally understand we should look out for ourselves, but there is a time when we must realize that others are more important than ourselves. That does not mean to neglect our own well-being, but our focus changes, for the good of everyone involved. The priority of looking at others differently and more important than yourself just works well and is proven by the principles of scripture. Philippians 2:23 (ESV) says that we are to "Do nothing from selfish ambition or conceit, but in humility count others as more significant than yourself."

The priority is to consider others first, after your relationship with God. When He is first, the priorities take care of themselves.

When I say that we are to get to the end of ourselves, we surrender to God and allow Him to take the reins of our lives, kind of get out of the way and submit. We come by faith to His priorities not ours. You can know His priorities by spending more time paying attention to what He says. I will talk more about how God speaks to us a little later in the book, but for now, just know that He wrote a book for us to learn about Him: The Bible. We use our experiences, knowledge and plans to build our own pride and that sometimes hinders Gods work through us. Humility before God is the beginning of wisdom from God. Coming to the end of ourselves is when God can begin to work in all areas of life.

You may have seen the bumper sticker that reads, "God is my co-pilot". I have news for you, He does not want you flying the plane. You have no training. We are not co-piloting in life with God. He is our pilot, and He can take the wheel. This attitude sets up a best-case scenario for our priorities. When we seek His will first, every area of life runs smoother, although the challenges do not disappear. He gave us gifts such as a family and the ability to work. He desires to bless those areas and so much more. When the priority is His, everything works much better. In Colossians 3:23-24 (NKJV) it reads: "And whatever you do, do it heartily, as to the Lord and not to men, knowing that from the Lord you will receive the reward of inheritance; for you serve the Lord Christ."

Allow God to bless you and those He puts in your life. You are not to separate yourself from God's work, pay attention, and commit to understand His design in you. Knowing more about His will while working in conjunction with His principles increases our knowledge of the character of Jesus Christ.

It takes consistent practice to allow God to work in your life as a priority. We practice our faith in all areas of our lives to grow with Him. Allow Him to work on your marriage and the upbringing of your children, your workplace relationships, and your social environment. You will know you are learning when you are experiencing joy and peace in all circumstances. Understand that the journey is not all roses, there will be challenges along the way. Practicing faith takes work, hard work that pays off with inner peace. We all desire inner peace. Practice makes permanent, not perfection. Developing faith takes perseverance, humility, and a yielding or surrender to the Spirit of God. I will get into these areas of growth and development a little further on in the book.

He Will Meet You Now

Begin your walk with the Lord today, right now. What are you waiting for? There is no better time to ask for His priorities, His peace, and His joy than today. If you are hurting inside, or just desire peace concerning decisions you need to make, ask Him for help. You may need to mend a long-term relationship. Life may seem to be falling apart. Now is a good time to take refuge, right where you are. Ask Him for direction in how to make Him a priority, as if you were speaking with a friend.

Pray something like this: "Lord, I need You, you designed me to have a strong relationship with You, but I have ignored that as a priority. I ask right now that You take over and show me Your ways, give me a peace about the direction You will have me follow. Forgive me for doing this life by myself without regard for You. I ask that You change my heart for the sake of Your Son Jesus." He just wants to hear your "Heart at Work" towards Him.

CHAPTER TWO

FORGIVENESS FROM THE HEART

Forgiving, and being forgiven, clears the path for the love of God to begin moving through your life. This was my first lesson with my new attitude.

Things Will Be Just Fine – I Thought

The traumatic experience I had on the road that Friday afternoon began a new life for me and my family. I had no idea what the future held or what was going to happen to my wife Janice and our children. The only thing I knew was that my mindset changed from thinking of myself to being careful that I thought about my wife and children. I wish I could say that it was an easy transition, but changes were going to take time and consistency. I had no idea what to expect from my newfound faith.

I thought everything was going to be better at home. I mean, I was not going out without my wife anymore. I stopped going to the refrigerator for a beer on the weekends and I was paying closer attention to the kids when I was home. Isn't that the way it should have been from the beginning? I was excited about life and the possibilities for the future.

Every Sunday, I was excited to go to church. I was hungry to hear about what the pastor talked about from the Bible. I bought my first Bible, and my faith was growing. I was reading the words every day for a few months. God was working in my heart, finally getting my priorities in order.

Houston, (or San Antonio), We Have a Problem.

It seemed like every Sunday, my wife and I had an argument about getting to church on time or having the kids ready to go. Why was it so hard to get to church on Sunday? My life had changed, and I was being a good husband and a decent dad. Janice should have been happy about that. We no longer argued about me going out on Friday night or not paying attention to our children.

Then one day, I was standing in the kitchen talking with Janice while she was watching TV. The kids were in the back bedroom playing. I asked her to look at me and answer this question, why was it so hard to get to church on Sunday? Why did we have to argue each week about one thing or another? I mean, I changed. God had changed my heart, forgiven me for my wrongdoings and put me on a good path, so I thought. Why couldn't she see this? Why the fight?

Have you ever seen the movie "The Exorcist"? It was a movie back in 1973 where a twelve-year-old girl is demon possessed. There was a scene when the girl turned her head 180 degrees to look at the priest. It was a scary part of the movie, believe me. I am not saying that my wife was demon possessed, but to me, that moment was in slow motion. Janice turned her head to me and said something that stopped me dead in my tracks. My mouth was stuck. She told me that she was glad that God had forgiven me for how I lived and that He changed my heart. She continued telling me that in all the years we had been married, the places we went, the troubles we had, not one time have I asked for her forgiveness for the way I treated her.

Remember the shock on the road when God changed my spirit? I am a guy who rarely was stuck for words, but I had nothing in response to her statement. It reminded me of just a few months before when the Spirit of God stopped me while I was driving home from work thinking of my trail ride. Honestly, my first thought was that Janice could never have thought of such a profound statement on her own. Where did she get the insight to make such a deep intuitive comment? Well, there goes God again working through my wife. I realized since that time that God can use whoever He wants to reach anyone, whenever and wherever he wants. He is God, I am not!

The Response

What happened next took our relationship to another level. I stood there for a few minutes, and then my legs moved towards her. My heart was pounding, my mind was focused as I walked up to her, without hesitation, got on my knees in front of her, soaking wet from crying eyes. I asked her to forgive me for my total disregard of her over the years. We sat for what seemed like an hour crying on each other's shoulders. This was a major turning point to our marriage relationship. The Spirit of God was all over us. It is important to understand that we would not have reconciled on our own. I was a prideful, stubborn man that needed a mighty hand of God to change my ways.

My heart was pierced by God and He led me to ask my wife for forgiveness. How many husbands, or wives for that matter, need to listen to God and ask for forgiveness from their spouses? I have told this story many times and the response has been overwhelming. Maybe there is someone reading this book who seems to have a good walk with the Lord, but your husband or wife is not on the same page. Now may be the time to ask for forgiveness for a past that has not been honorable to the Lord or your spouse.

Men, have you been the leader God intended you to be? Ladies, have you honored the Lord by allowing your husband to be a Godly leader, or have you taken the leadership role upon yourself? Now would be a good time to evaluate those relationships and assure that priorities are in line. Go first to the Lord for forgiveness, then to the one you hurt unintentionally. Once your priorities are made right, God will bless the entire household for generations to come.

God began a work in my wife and me as a married couple. He opened the doors to our future personal development and spiritual growth. I am reminded in the Bible that I should have my house in order. It was not in order. In Joshua 24:15 (NKJV) it says, "as for me and my house we will serve the Lord". I was the leader of my house and my wife was a vital link in honoring and serving the Lord. Our children could be raised in the admonition of the Lord when both of us serve Him together with honor.

Are You Really Married?

After I asked my wife for forgiveness, my heart was changed, and we began our true walk together. Sundays were smoother, and we began to work together to get the kids ready for church. That was another area of growth for me, helping Janice with the house and the children. I took her for granted more times than I would like to admit. That is still a work in progress.

Without getting into all the details, Janice recommitted her life to the Lord just months after our reconciliation. Our oldest daughter decided to follow Jesus at the same time. I am happy to report that they both are serving the Lord with gladness along with our other two grown children. Janice is a dedicated wife and mom of our three adult children and grandmother to ten grandchildren. She is passionate about pouring herself into them with all her heart, mind, and soul.

The day we reconciled, three transformational seeds were planted in me that I had to water, feed, and nurture.

Seed 1- The first seed that must be sown is **Humility.** Pride can destroy any relationship very quickly. Allow God to use you with the recognition of self-righteousness.

Seed 2- The next seed would be to **Listen;** listen well. Listen to God and listen to your spouse, and anyone else who speaks peace and life into your heart.

Seed 3- **Action** - Follow up under the leading of The Spirit of God. Allow Him to work through you to give away your heart to others, especially your spouse.

What seeds are you tending?

The Power of Forgiveness

What does it mean to totally forgive someone? What is forgiveness and what is not forgiveness? And what is a disguise of forgiveness? Beginning with an understanding that we are all broken people that need help with life, forgiveness is the truest meaning of love. Every single person, despite upbringing, social status, moral fortitude, or self-sufficiency, needs a Savior. God designed us to need Him.

Forgiveness starts from your heart, translates into your mind, and spills out with your actions. It is a total regard for the person to be forgiven. There must be no personal pride on behalf of the forgiver. It is a clear understanding that the person that is forgiven is forgiven because God would do the same.

Forgiveness is not about you. It is not bringing back the past of the person forgiven. That is not real forgiveness. Pointing to the flaws of others does absolutely nothing for a forgiving spirit. People will have different personalities so accept people where they are. Forgiveness is not continued resentment.

Sometimes, it looks like you forgive someone for something they did against you when you see them face to face, but deep down inside, resentment can eat you up. The outside looks good, but inside is what the Bible calls like dirty rags, keeping you from loving another person.

Before we continue, who is someone God is inviting you to forgive? Keep them in mind for the rest of this chapter. Many people carry around grudges, hate, disregard, and unforgiveness for others. It may be close to home with family members or longtime friends that hurt your relationship. Who comes to mind? Is it someone that you have not spoken to in years? Is it someone who did something that you said could never be forgiven? I know I am getting personal, but that is my intention. Name the person who you have not forgiven. Picture the person without regard to the circumstances. They may have a history of evil behavior; they may have hurt a family member or someone close to you. I want you to think of that person while we look at the scripture and see how forgiveness played a role in the lives of others.

The first example is Jesus. Jesus is the ultimate example of forgiveness. He died so that we could, would, and should forgive. Despite His circumstances of death on the cross, He forgave his executioners, even though He did not deserve to die a heartless death because He did nothing wrong. The example of Jesus should be enough for all of us to realize how important forgiveness is to bring to the cross, despite any circumstances. Our heart should be pierced in such a way that forgiveness becomes a natural response to any transgression against us.

In the first book of the Bible, we find the story of a family fractured and restored: Joseph, in Genesis, Chapter 50, is being blessed as God's special messenger. Jacob, his father, told Joseph about his future. Joseph told his brothers and that was all they needed to plot His death. They were remarkably jealous of their brother's success and the special treatment by their father, so they brought him to the desert to die. But God had other plans. He not only saved him from death by starvation but brought Joseph to a prominent position in the kingdom. Here is what the scripture says **Joseph** said to them: (Gen 50:19-21) NKJV "Do not be afraid, for *am* I in the place of God? But as for you, you meant evil against me; *but* God meant it for good, to bring it about as *it is* this day, to save many people alive. Now therefore, do not be afraid; I will provide for you and your little ones." And he comforted them and spoke kindly to them despite their intention to end his life.

Do you have jealousy in your heart towards someone? Is there envy in your heart about the success of someone you know? What is stopping you from forgiving someone?

You may have heard of the story of The Prodigal Son in Luke 15:11-32. There was a man who had two sons. One was older than the other and the younger one decided that he had enough and wanted to get away. So, he went to his father and asked for his inheritance to get him started. We all know that an inheritance is something we get when the father dies and the promise to pass something down goes into effect. The father granted the younger son the money and the son left for a foreign land. Now, the older son stayed home with his father. It appears the older son did not mind staying under the father's roof. He had everything he needed and more.

This is played out many times when a teenager wants to get away from their parents and go on their own, leaving the protection of God's chosen people in their parents.

As expected, the younger son spent all the money and fell on some really hard times. He found himself begging on the streets for food or whatever he could get his hands on to survive. He ended up eating the pig slop on a business owner's property - just to get something in his stomach.

He did what he wanted to do on his own terms, but he soon realized that he had made a big mistake. He had it made at his father's house. He had everything he needed and many of the things he wanted.

Sound Familiar? We do the same thing. Don't we take for granted many of the blessings we have? I certainly do, at times. Eventually, this son came to the end of himself. He began to think of how his father had servants who were treated far better than he was right then. So, he planned on going back to his father. He knew he had to humble himself before him and make the relationship right again.

As a parent, we want nothing more for our children than to be blessed. We direct them with wisdom and try to keep them out of harm's way, so their lives will be spared. We want only the best for them. The young son started on his journey back to the life he had before, with a contrite heart and spirit.

Amazing Grace Displayed

His father was waiting for him with open arms. Even though his son went away and disgraced his father and family, he was waiting to welcome him back with a warm embrace. He already had forgiven him for the harm he did to the family name.

Here are a couple of significant principles we can take out of this story:

1. What we need in life is right in front of us, yet we take it for granted. My family was right in front of me, but I was looking for something different, something more satisfying, or something I thought would be better than what I had with my family. So, I found myself running away from my circumstances.

2. God brought me back, only when I humbled myself and submitted to the Father. We are not robots that God directs without our own will. He only accepts us into the fold when we come willingly and broken. When we are broken, He can begin the healing process. If we think we are whole in ourselves only, He will not force His will on us. We are broken vessels that need a Healer.

There are many broken people in workplaces and churches all around the world. "A humble spirit to a proud disposition can neutralize pride and prompt humility." We have opportunities all day long to pass on the attitude of a humble spirit, so that the influence we have will have an impact on those around us.

When we forgive someone in the real sense, like forgiving them because they did not realize what they were doing, it gives an overwhelming peace to the forgiver. Forgiveness takes the weight off our shoulders. The biggest part of forgiveness is that the forgiver is free to love the person they forgive. They can now look at the person differently, without the burden of the offense reminding them of how bad they are.

For the one being forgiven, they will see that the forgiver has changed their disposition towards them and that things in the relationship are improving. A good thing to keep in mind at this point is that the person forgiven may not realize they wronged you. Showing them, they are forgiven instead of telling them how they hurt you will produce better results. Allow them to think about their own behavior as your relationship strengthens.

Unforgiveness Keeps on Taking

How can withholding forgiveness from your spouse impact your relationship? The biggest problem with unforgiveness toward a spouse, or anyone for that matter, but especially a spouse, is that unforgiveness affects every area of your life. If you do not forgive your spouse, the intimacy you have with them will be affected. The subject of the hurt will always be on your mind. You cannot be intimate with your spouse when the focus is on the hurt. You can play the part for a period, maybe, but there will still be a wall to full restoration. How do you make love to someone when you cannot love them the way they are intended to be loved, unconditionally? Isn't the intimacy skewed? The only question you will have is, how long will it go on that way? The longer it goes on, the deeper the root grows, and that root can turn into bitterness. Cut the root!

Overall, with many people, our conversations are superficial. There is no depth in a conversation unless both people desire for that to happen. With our spouse, it must be different. Our conversations must be more intimate, revealing, and appealing. If we have something against someone, especially our spouse, the relationship will not progress. It will continue to diminish.

The impact and influence we can have on our spouse (or anyone else) will surely be affected by our attitude. The time you spend with someone will eventually reveal what is going on inside you. One thing to keep in mind is what comes out of your mouth in conversation and attitude will carry from your heart what you believe about the person you are speaking to. If you still have unforgiveness in your heart and mind, sooner or later, it will rear its ugly head in your attitude. Be aware how unforgiveness works and forgive quickly! You have no time to waste.

Why should you forgive your spouse before all others? Because this is the perfect place to start. In the book of Genesis, God describes what happens when two people marry under His design. They leave mommy and daddy and are joined together so much so that they become one flesh. Gen 2:24. They are joined to develop such an intimate relationship that they cannot be broken without killing the design. When we are joined to a spouse in holy matrimony, anything that hinders that growth, hurts the relationship with both people.

When unforgiveness or hurt is not addressed quickly, it will hinder a couple's growth in every way. Staying in constant awareness of our brokenness with the willingness of a forgiving spirit is vital to the growth of your marriage. The Holy Spirit will help you and your spouse do things you are not able to do on your own.

If you are married, you have a responsibility to develop a stronger bond in fulfillment of God's design for an eternal relationship together with Him. This is our first responsibility. From there we can impact the lives of others. Your testimony will benefit everyone else dealing with the unforgiveness issue.

Forgiving, and being forgiven by your spouse clears the path for the love of God to begin moving in and through your life. Always remember, you have a helper. God will be with you as you do uncomfortable things.

CHAPTER THREE
HEALING OF THE HEART

Janice and I were living a good life. We had three beautiful children: two teenage girls and a ten-year-old boy. I had retired from the Air Force to begin graduate school at Southeastern Seminary in Wake Forest, NC. I learned plenty about life in those days. I was wrapped up in ministry and education and home each day with my family. Our daughters explored all kinds of avenues, both good and bad. Our middle daughter proved to be more independent as she grew in her teenage years. These years were most challenging for my wife and me. We traveled every three years with our family. It was hard for my kids making new friends at each assignment. We did not realize that it certainly affected the way they looked at things. One of the most difficult times of our lives had to do with our middle daughter.

We believe there was a time one of her friends told her since she was sixteen, she did not have to listen to her parents anymore. We still are not sure what turned on the fire hydrant of misbehavior, but things changed in our house. We were involved in a local church, so most of the time, our kids had a group of friends their age.

You must have heard about pastors' children... how they are usually more boisterous than other children. Not sure why, but there are certainly challenges along the way, while raising children in a faith-based home.

Our middle child was challenging us in every direction for about two years, from fourteen to sixteen, at least. She would do the opposite of what we would say. If we told her, she could not wear the clothes she had on, she would find clothes that were further away from the standard we set. She hung out with friends from school that were bad influences on her from day one. She was more of a follower than a leader. We certainly saw glimpses of leadership potential at times, but her so-called friends were also trying to figure life out on their own.

As the days passed, her anger towards us intensified radically. She rebelled around every turn. Many times, it seemed that everything was a fight. A fight that we were not prepared to tackle. The battles continued almost daily, with the intensity increasing. There were a few times when the police had to be called to our home. Our oldest daughter and our son were affected in a big way. Her behavior was hurting everyone in her path.

We knew something had to be done and done quickly. She could not stay in the house any longer. We made an extremely hard and sad decision to send her to a short-term home for rebellious troubled girls called the House of Hope. To this day sending her away from the house was the hardest decision we made in our lives. I cry when I think about it. We knew that it could only help, she was a very smart girl that could manipulate with the best of them. We could see the potential in her, but she was misdirected at the time. We felt helpless, all we could do is give her to the Lord and be there when called upon.

As a dad, I was trying to get her to see that her actions were hurtful, but she would have none of that. I wrote her letters all the time. The reason I wrote letters was because we could not have a civil conversation about anything. If you have a strong-willed teenager, you may understand to some degree. Talking exploded into a tsunami quickly because we both had hard heads that clashed often under most circumstances. I would say "No," she would say "Yes!" Her rebellion was out of control.

I remember times when I would take her on trips just to spend time with her. She would accept the trip but not the conversation. I wanted to let her know that her behavior was unacceptable towards her parents. We did everything we knew to get her to accept responsibility for her actions.

Redemption for Real

She did well in the House of Hope and excelled in everything she did, playing the game well. She graduated with flying colors and came home only to continue to rebel. This time, just a bit smarter and more manipulative.

Can you relate to some of what has happened to us as parents? We went through a living hell with our daughter for a period of about three years. Our oldest daughter went to Liberty University for part of it and our son stayed with us throughout the whole adventure. I know every one of us was affected in various ways.

Fast forward a few years, our oldest daughter came back from Liberty University, met a young godly man and is raising five children. Our son is happily married to a beautiful, godly woman and they have three boys. Our middle daughter joined the Air Force and served honorably for four years. When she got out, she moved to Louisiana then Massachusetts. Then she came here to Nashville and finished her bachelor's degree in design. She has now settled down in this area with a solid husband and two children. God is good all the time.

I felt as though we were robbed of many good times. We are responsible for the upbringing of our children. There is a scripture in Proverbs 22:6 (NLT) "Direct your children onto the right path, and when they are older, they will not leave it." That part of scripture was a goal for us to see come to fruition. Even though the times were hard, we did what we knew. As a parent, we make plenty of mistakes and there are times I wish I would have acted differently. We cannot take them back, but we can go forward. That is what we did.

For years, whenever I thought of my middle daughter, I would get angry. She had no idea how much pain she caused everyone in our family. Her behavior during the three years in North Carolina was like a lifetime of damage. I had a hard time with this for years after it was over. I watched her continue to make bad decisions in life, but she would not listen to wise direction. I just could not forget or forgive until I came to the end of myself regarding forgiveness. Learning how to forgive is hard and constant.

The Hurt Would Not Leave

The sun was shining strong one day in mid-June. I was sitting in my car outside a funeral home waiting to go in to visit a friend's family member. I was praying for my family, especially my daughter. She was in the Air Force. She was having a hard time with several areas of life. I was writing her a letter, as I did often, just to tell her that I cared about her and the decisions she was making.

As I was praying, God revealed a truth to me that changed the way I looked at forgiveness. Honestly, I was thinking about Jesus on the cross being crucified. He was dying a slow painful death; both the Romans and the Jews were watching this spectacle. Crucifixion was without a doubt the most agonizing way to die in that day. It was a way in which criminals were tortured. Many of the people in the crowd wanted to see him suffer, others did not. Picture this: Jesus is bleeding, his whole body is in excruciating pain and what does He say? **"Father forgive them for they do not know what they do". (Luke 23:34) NKJV.**

The implications of His words are far reaching. Forgive them for they do not know how this is going to affect everyone. They do not know that what they are doing will bring salvation to all that believe. They do not know how many people will be affected by their actions. They really do not have a clue what is ahead.

These words pierced my heart. I needed to forgive my daughter. She did not know how much her behavior hurt her mother or father or her sister or brother. As many teenagers, they think only of only themselves. I was there, were you? She had no idea that I would have to learn about forgiveness for a lifetime. She did not know that I would learn how to love her better than ever before.

Jesus – Vital Key to Forgiveness

Here is a key ingredient that must be taken into consideration: I could not love my daughter until I forgave her behavior. Whenever I thought about her in unforgiveness, I did not love her. There was a brick wall stopping me from loving her because of her actions. I did not even like her, never mind love her like I should.

It would not have done me any good to tell her that I forgive her because she would have just told me that we as parents caused the problem to begin with and our actions exasperated her behavior. So, I just forgave her inside my heart.

I was able to love her from that point on. I did not say I wanted to hang out with her or even have a long dialogue with her. As a matter of fact, I did not. From that point on, I just told her that I loved her, and I will do anything she needed. I did not pursue her acceptance. I released her into the Lord's hands.

Freedom to Press Forward

There is a freedom in forgiveness that gives peace, no matter what happens to those that you forgive. Once you release the person to the Lord, you have done what Jesus did. He forgave those that hurt Him, that killed Him, that crucified Him.

The change that occurs in forgiveness is freedom and peace. There is no better release. There is no more bondage. We look at the people we forgave from the Lord's perspective. If they are loved, they may come to experience change in their lives.

People want to be loved. God is love. He loved the world enough to "give His only Son, so that if we would believe in Him, we would have eternal life" with Him in heaven, John 3:16. That is love in the purest sense.

We Cannot Change People

It is not up to us to change the behavior of the person who has wronged you. That is God's job, and He gets pleasure seeing people come to Him. We can be an influence that God uses to change a person's attitude towards others. We can be influential as ambassadors to see God work. We influence, He changes!

Newness and Peace

Forgiveness has brought us all freedom from the bondage of chaos. We have witnessed a remarkable change in the life of our middle daughter. She is still hard-headed like her father, but she thinks through most circumstances now before reacting to a situation. Her relationship with her Lord is growing each day and she has relied on His grace and mercy often in life's continued challenges. Surely, she and I can love better than before.

Who Do You Think You Are? - Living and Forgiving

What does the Bible tell us about living in a forgiven state? The question becomes, who do we think we are when we do not forgive someone for their trespasses?

Scripture tells us, we are forgiven by the sacrificial shed blood of Jesus Christ on the cross. He purposely died so that we could live, living a life of forgiveness, as He did. Ephesians 1:7(ESV) "In him we have redemption through his blood, the forgiveness of our trespasses, according to the riches of his grace,"

Forgiveness is a way of life. Forgiveness should happen often with the realization that it can have an impact on the lives of others for years to come. Here are some steps that can help you to forgive others and evaluate where you are in your relationship with God.

Step 1: Evaluate where you are in your relationship with God

We need to begin the forgiving process by looking at ourselves and allowing the forgiveness to begin with us. We must know we have no control over the people that caused us harm with their actions or their words, only influence.

Start with prayer. Just take some time alone with God and ask for help. You were hurt and that is never easy. It begins with having a soft heart towards your offender.

We are not God; God changes lives every day. We live in a world of broken people that need to be loved. We can love them despite them just as God loves us despite us.

Step 2: Think through the damage and all the folks involved

Be an influencer: People will see your actions towards others and listen to words of forgiveness from your own mouth. They see your heart's actions. People can be influenced, rather than forcibly changed.

Make it a point to speak to others about how important forgiveness can be for them and the possibility of lives and hearts being changed.

God is the author of forgiveness. If you follow the example set by our great God, you will be released from the bondage of unforgiveness. Many times, the forgiveness (and unforgiveness) affects other people outside your sphere of influence, whether they know it or not. People watch and listen how believers act in word and deed.

Step 3: Allow God to continue to love other people as He does

God loves you despite what you say or do to Him or the people that have hurt you. He will love those you forgive. The evidence will show.

Really, the only thing you can do practically is soften your heart towards the offender. Understand and go speak to the person who hurt you. If you speak to them, you do not have to bring up the hurt. When you have been hurt, it is hard to look at the person that hurt you and forget about the offense. That will be the challenge that only God can do for you.

Real forgiveness is a gift from God. He is the only one that can teach real forgiveness based on His sacrificial shedding of blood on the cross. The more we know about the character of God in Jesus, the more we will understand how to interact with others with a forgiving heart.

Let it B.U.R.N. Inside – Forgiveness Action Plan

Beginning – Start with a self-evaluation of your heart attitude. Do I have a forgiving spirit? Do I understand that we all are broken people to some degree? We all have a unique story to tell. We all have been hurt one time or another by other people. Once we understand the brokenness, we will begin to understand how God can heal us from the inside out, only then can we forgive.

Urgency – Hurry, life goes by way too fast. We do not have time to stay enemies with others. Unforgiveness is unhealthy, it affects us physically, mentally, and spiritually. Life is precious, there must be a strong urgency not to hold on to unforgiveness for too long, hurting everyone in its path.

Refinement – Healing begins with a practice of forgiveness from God's perspective. "Father forgive them for they know not what they do." Luke 23:34 (KJV) Get better at forgiveness, study forgiveness as if your life depends on practicing its principles.

Newness – Experience this freedom from the bondage of unforgiveness, freedom to love the way we are intended and designed to love others, despite their faults, recognizing our own inadequacies and God's forgiveness in us.

What will happen in your life when you begin to forgive people (whether you tell them or not) right now? Here are four final points to ponder:

1. **What you will notice in your spirit** – There will be no more tension when the name of the offender comes up in conversation or thought. You will experience a joy of forgiveness in your heart, and you will be thankful to God that you can forgive as He forgives you.

2. **What you will notice in your mind** – You will be thinking of the possibilities in the future of the way you act towards other people. You will not be so easily offended by the words and actions of others.

3. **What you will notice in your emotions** – Your emotions will be thought out, your character will be sweetened, your disposition will be pleasant, and your discernment of healthy relationships will become clearer. You won't fly into an emotional state right away. You'll know the truth about forgiveness, and you will not be the same.

4. **Other ways** – Your life perspective about people will be changed. I did not say that it would be easy, people are not easy - remember the brokenness! Once we

understand that most people do not have a healthy idea of forgiveness, it will be our responsibility to influence that change in the lives of others. We will become more valuable to others and at peace with our God.

CHAPTER FOUR

DEPRESSION OF THE HEART

Depression is real. Do not let it get the best of you! I am convinced that we are not designed to handle more than a few significant emotional situations at the same time by ourselves. Life can get dark and our vision for a bright future can be skewed when we keep the light out. Even in your darkest moments, God is with you.

Crazy Times Can Sneak up on You – "Am I Worth It?"

The weeks were passing faster than the days. Time stops for no one. My mind was racing as I began my trip home. I was not at the top of my game all day long. Too many things were happening at one time and my thoughts were all over the place. My walk with the Lord was strong, my attitude was positive. I realize that I have little to no control over the circumstances or people outside of decisions I make and what influence I can pass on. The previous three weeks had been considerably emotional. I had officiated two funerals and attended two more as an invited guest of families.

I do get emotional often in my older age. I tend to take things to heart when a sad story, or for that matter, a story of joyous victory is told. I was still broken by being fired from a job for the first time in my life. That happened just six months prior. I wasn't thinking much about that, but I guess it was in my subconscious at the time.

I really believed God had me in a good place by allowing me to be trained with a mission to reach people in the work-place to a hopeful future. I knew there were plenty of broken people like me in the corporate world and beyond. I didn't realize just how broken I was until I walked in the door that day. My wife met me at the door and asked a question that was not at all threatening or confrontational. I just looked at her and said, "Just leave me alone." It was odd for me to speak to Janice with such abruptness.

My behavior was very unusual towards my wife, Janice. She just backed up and I went about my business. She left me alone. I felt a very heavy burden that I had never experienced before. I wanted to just stick my head in a hole. Sitting on a chair in my bedroom with the door closed, my heart was racing faster than normal. My mind was filtering through my relationships with my wife, my children, grandchildren, and the personal relationships I had with people in ministry. Something was happening and I did not like what I was feeling.

I looked over at the dresser and thought for a minute that I should open the drawer and take out the .38 pistol and end my life with one shot. Wow! It scared me so much, that in one single instant, I could think of such a tragic ending to a life full of joy.

I remember when my mother was sent to the hospital because she could not breathe. The doctors told her that her lungs were full of damage and she needed to quit smoking. That scared her so much, she instantly stopped, and lived a good number of years after her scare.

Similarly, I really got scared and immediately called out to God. I am so glad that I knew Him personally. He has taken me through some rough waters before and I knew He would carry me through this.

I could no longer think about ending my life. I felt His presence with me from that minute on. I ran to get my Bible and began reading. I went directly to the book of Psalms. I knew enough about that book that God would honor my time searching for just the right words – the words He used for David during His struggles. I must have read about fifty of the one hundred and fifty Psalms, only to be lifted in countenance to a place of peace.

I sat there for a little bit longer, realizing that what I encountered just minutes before was evil. More importantly, I realized that during that whole encounter, I had to stop and think for a minute, leaving the emotions aside and go to the One who created me for Him, Jesus Christ. He said He would not leave me or forsake me, and again, it proved to be true.

I had studied and encountered spiritual warfare on more than one occasion during my walk with God. This was powerful beyond anything I had ever experienced. Ephesians 6:12 (NLT) "For we are not fighting against flesh-and-blood enemies, but against evil rulers and authorities of the unseen world, against mighty powers in this dark world, and against evil spirits in the heavenly places." This was hitting too close to home. I sat there for another few minutes, then immediately went to find Janice. I sat down with her and told the story of what I was thinking. I had no idea that I could get to this depth of despair. A depressive spirit like that had never occurred in me to that degree. Never had I experienced such a down moment to the point of ending my life. I know that we all get depressed to some degree, but most of the time, we get out of it and press on with life. This time was different.

The Bible is clear that God created us to have fellowship with Him. The Word is also clear that we will have trouble in this world. In John 16:33 (NKJV) it tells what Jesus said, He knew people would be scattered when the time came for Him to go through the torment leading up to the cross. He stated, "These things I have spoken to you, that in Me you may have peace, In the world you will have tribulation; but be of good cheer, I have overcome the world." Say AMEN!

Why Are We All Broken?

We are broken because we are all human, and we are not designed to go through this world without our Creator, Jesus Christ. He created us to need a Savior. He was sent so that salvation would come through Him.

No one is perfect. Jesus was the only perfect human being. He did not sin (separate from God) because He was God in the flesh. If He sinned at all, he would not be God. A sinful god cannot perfect a sinful man. A pure, sinless God can bring sinful man into union with Him and make Him pure in His very being. That is what He did on the cross of Calvary. Trusting by faith in what Jesus Christ did for all of us as broken human beings can save us from eternity apart from Him. We will be with Him for eternity. **"For God was pleased to have all his fullness dwell in him, and through him to reconcile to himself all things, whether things on earth or things in heaven, by making peace through his blood, shed on the cross". Colossians 1:19-20 (NKJV)**

No one would know what I thought that day unless I told them, as I am telling you in this book. People would look at me and speak with me without any idea what I was thinking. I dress neatly, I speak articulately most of the time, and I have a super friendly personality. We meet people all day long and only get a glimpse of who they are from the outside. Our interactions are superficial at best. This should teach us a lesson about not judging a person by what we see on the outside. This story reiterates that principle...

A Book by Its Cover

I am reminded of when I first began my work as a Chaplain/ Pastor for a trucking company. I was brand new to this location and I had to introduce myself to all the employees. To be honest, I was a bit intimidated by some of the truckers I met. DJ was one of them. He was about 6'3" and 300 pounds, with a bunch of muscles. He had a dark beard that just added to the scare. I saw him getting out of his 53-foot tractor trailer as I began my walk up to him to introduce myself. I was self-assured, but for some reason, this guy intimidated me. Well, I approached him cautiously, introduced myself, and explained why I was on the yard. I told him that I was here to serve the people in this location as the Chaplain. I'll never forget what he did, he just smiled and gave me a big hug. That was the beginning of a great relationship. I am telling you this story to illustrate that it is not what you see on the outside that is important. It is what is going on inside that is vital to us building lasting, long-term relationships. I became good friends with DJ, a friendship that lasted until his untimely death in a motorcycle crash (he had a heart attack) two years after we met. I had the privilege of speaking at his funeral; a day I will never forget.

The day I thought about ending my life changed my direction forever. I hope this real-life situation will give hope to anyone who reads about the impact. My story, like yours, can have a great impact on other people. No matter how tragic the circumstances, we never know just how close people are to giving up on life. We hear about it all the time: a well-known actor, pastor, friend, or family member who committed suicide. We're surprised and saddened. It looked as though they had a good life from the outside. They had money, a good family, lots of friends, and a good reputation as far as we knew, from the outside. But, inside, people struggle all day long, all the time! Many times, we have no idea what people are thinking on the inside unless we invest ourselves in getting to know them on a deeper level - dig deeper if they allow you.

Life passes us quickly. Invest in the lives of those you love. Open your heart towards them and chances are, they will open their heart to you when they need you most. Make it your mission to build deeper relationships at home and in your place of work, dig deeper.

Lots of Hurting People

I am writing this book in the middle of a global pandemic. A virus is wreaking havoc with the world and many people are scared for their lives. People are hurting themselves at a rate never seen in our history. There are about 38,000 people who kill themselves each year. In 2020, that number increased substantially because of the pandemic. The American Foundation for Suicide Prevention says that there are about 132 people per day that die by suicide. That is a tragedy. Surely, something can be done when we realize the value in human life to our Lord and pass on that value. There may be times when you feel that all hope is gone, but that is not the way God thinks of you. You and I were created with a purpose that needs to be exercised.

If we would spend more time with people whom we come in contact within the workplace, the church, social environments, schools, and any other places where people gather, we could stop someone committing suicide.

I do understand that there is such a thing as mental illness. This illness is real. People from all walks of life struggle with mental issues each day. But according to the Center for Disease Control, over 60% of suicides were not people who have been treated for a mental illness.

The lives that we touch will touch other lives and on and on. We certainly have a responsibility to get to know people personally and intimately. God designed us to help each other.

Someone told me recently, "Well Tom, I have an uncle and a couple of cousins that killed themselves and my grandfather committed suicide in the early 80's. We have this type of behavior in our family. It seems like generations carry this gene." A gene for suicide or depression is far beyond my educational level. I can only speak from the relational level.

Our personal experiences are different from others. Each of us has a family background with varying educational and mental capacity. We all are in different places regarding our relationship with The Lord. If I did not have a relationship with the Lord when I contemplated suicide, things would certainly be different. My pride may have affected the way I looked at the whole situation. I would have certainly dealt with my circumstances differently. It would have been about me, not about those I loved.

I have no idea what would have happened if things were different. We cannot think about that. Life is what it is for you. You and I bring our stories to life in real time through our histories, experiences, and family makeup. Our generations' DNA and many other factors all add up to life as we know it now.

In the chapters ahead I will share with you some proven strategies to avoid getting to the point of taking your own life. This may be helpful for anyone going through a depressive time. Prevention is key to keeping people from going so far into a pit that they feel they cannot climb out. You can be there for someone if you understand something about prevention. God has a purpose and a plan for each of us, are we listening?

We must come face to face with the reality of depression or even the thought of suicide. There are literally hundreds of scriptures that specifically cover God's view of us as believers in Jesus. They are personal because He is a personal God. You are valuable and you can be used mightily by God for His glory.

Losing Heart - Why Are You Feeling Down?

Let me make something clear about depression. Keep in mind that I am not a medical practitioner or a licensed psychologist or psychiatrist. I am a Pastor with over twenty years of experience interacting with thousands of people, helping many get through life's difficult times. That is all. I'm just a guy called by God. Trained to serve people while coming alongside them when they break. The way I look at my role is that God must direct my path every step of the way. I do that by getting closer with my Lord. I do that by reading the Bible very often, at least part of every day. Bible study should be on purpose with the intention of gleaning wisdom and truth by faith. My faith, plus my interaction with people who are suffering, has taught me plenty, with more to come. Let us look at some of the reasons that people may get into a depressive state.

The following reasons are specific and relatively common as to why and how people like you and I can get into a depressive state:

Reason 1 – Terminal or Serious Health Issues

We are extremely limited without our health. If we have been diagnosed with a life-threatening illness or have a serious injury that changed the course of our lives, then we could get depressed rather easily. There may be a change in the way you have to live. Limitations that were never there before, getting used to the life changes, will often lead to a depressive state. I cannot tell you how many people that I visited in the hospital that had a great amount of money. What I can tell you is that their money was not that important at the time of their unhealthy situation.

We all have a lifestyle that we lead. Depending on our age, we settle into a way of life and get used to that way. When a major change occurs, the change can put us into a tailspin. Life will change if we are seriously hurt or get diagnosed with a debilitating illness, such as terminal cancer. Mentally and physically, things will be different. We will have to deal with many factors we did not have before outside of the illness. Depending on our social and family support (or lack of), people can lose heart easily and get into a state of depression that is difficult to overcome. Becoming sensitive to the subtle indicators of depression can be extremely helpful for others.

There are obvious signs of depression, such as separation from other people or changes in behavior. The changes will be obvious to those who are closest to the depressed person, such as a family member or spouse. Many times, a depressed person will become recluse, not wanting to be involved in any activities outside their comfort zone.

Be watchful and sensitive to sudden changes of behavior in people who have had deviations in their lives due to an injury or a life-threatening diagnosis. The better you know how they would normally act, the better you will know the changes. Do you know them well enough to approach them in love? You both have everything to gain and nothing to lose by approaching them with your concern. Show your heart to them! That action is "Hearts at Work."

Reason 2 – Loss of A Loved One

Another reason we can get depressed is when we lose someone we love. In a marriage relationship when a couple has been married for several years, one spouse dies, and the other spouse feels like they have no reason to live any longer. This is a particular issue with elderly people who have been married for a long time. They can fall into a state of depression. The sadness can take a toll on the living spouse.

Whenever someone close to you dies, it affects all the people they knew to some degree. The degree will depend on the depth of the relationship.

When we lose someone, we love, we never forget about them. We allow time to pass while remembering what they meant to us for the time we spent with them. Our memories are clear and lifelong. People deal with the loss in different ways, depending on the relationship. I recommend to people who have lost a loved one to wait about a year to either go into another relationship or make major decisions. It is important to take some time to heal. They may seek to fill the void quickly, which is not necessarily healthy. The loss of a spouse takes time to heal. Any loss takes time to heal from the inside out.

Reason 3 – Drugs or Alcohol Abuse

This is more common than you would think. There are more drug and alcohol abusers now because there are more drugs than ever before. In the middle of a pandemic, state and local governments had to determine what services were essential so that we could get a chance to starve the virus that has infiltrated the world. The government decided that liquor stores were essential to the community because, if they closed them, our hospitals would be overrun with people having alcohol withdrawal symptoms. After a quick search on the internet, I found at least one hundred different drugs that treat depression. (Drugs.com) What does that tell you? Obviously, there is a problem with depression in people. The pandemic of depression is increasing daily.

Many people feel that they are not capable of handling significant emotional events in their lives, so, they dull the pain with drugs or alcohol. The feelings of desperation last longer than the drugs or alcohol, so we do it again. Drugs and alcohol will control us, instead of us controlling the drugs or alcohol.

Watch for signs that people display. Personality change is a major indicator that something such as drugs or alcohol is altering a person's state of mind. It will seem abnormal for a person on drugs or alcohol to act unlike themselves in an altered state. Keep an eye on your loved ones.

Awareness of the people we are closest to will help us identify and reach out to people in trouble. I must repeat this - we have nothing to lose and everything to gain in helping a loved one. Reach out and do not get discouraged by the person's rejection if that happens. They need help from outside themselves.

From a spiritual standpoint: What would Jesus tell a depressed person if He was in that specific moment with them? He would tell them about their worth. First, He would tell them, "For I know the plans I have for you," says the LORD. "They are plans for good and not for disaster, to give you a future and a hope". Jerimiah 29:11 (NLT). Jesus would tell them that He knows exactly where they are in their lives with a full understanding of depression. He would tell them that He was sacrificed on the cross just for them individually.

Put your name in this scripture: For God so loved _____, that He gave His only son that if _____ would believe in Him, _____ would have everlasting life (John 3:16). Not only that but to have an abundant life here on earth. (John 10:10)

Whether they have a terminal illness or a disability that changes lives, people are meant to impact other people. God will use you and me to help others if we are willing to be used. We are to live life to the fullest so that others see our Lord through us.

Renewal and Refreshing

If someone is struggling with suicidal thoughts, what are their next best steps to keep moving forward and be renewed? Let me share a story with you.

In late June, the trucking industry is usually moving freight fast and furious. I thought to myself, this is a good time in this country. Whenever you see trucks on the road, even though they can be intimidating to drive next to while riding in a car, having truckers on the road is a good thing. It means the economy is moving well, and goods and services are active. Think of them as a blessing.

When I was serving as the Chaplain/Pastor for a major trucking company, I would try to interact with all the employees on a weekly basis. Making friends and building strong bonds with the people at work was a priority. One late afternoon, I received a call from a dock supervisor asking me to get to the terminal as soon as possible. His voice relayed a sense of urgency, so I hurried. I had to get some idea, so I asked if anyone was hurt, he just told me that one of the employees was threatening to kill himself with a gun. When I arrived, I was directed to the back of the dock to a 53-foot empty trailer. Mike was in the fetal position in the back. I immediately recognized him, so he allowed me to sit down next to him. It did not take long to interact because of the relationship. He trusted me, and for that, I am grateful.

My objective is always to make sure people are safe. I looked around, sat close to him and we began to talk about what he told his supervisor. I asked him what he said, and he told me exactly what the supervisor relayed to me. He was going to shoot himself. I asked where the gun was and when he intended on doing it. I talked to him for about 45 minutes to find out that he did not have a gun with him or in the car. He had to go to his father's house to get a gun. All I was trying to do was to see how real the immediate threat was to himself and others. We never know until we ask questions about the intentions. Many times, if they know you care for them, they will share what is going on in their heads. He knew that I was there to help him, so I gained immediate permission to help.

Mike agreed to allow me to take him to the closest hospital to get checked out, just so he'd feel better. We calmly walked out of the terminal and went to the hospital that was only five minutes down the road. I sat in the hospital with him for about three hours until his family arrived, and he was in good hands. He assured me that he would not try to take his life and that he felt better. I left the hospital and checked on him the next day. He was released under the care of his family that evening.

The doctors had determined that the medications he was taking were putting him into a tailspin. He seemed to be getting worse, so he wanted the pain to end. They identified the medication and changed it to a different brand and a lower dose. He stayed out of work for about a week until he was stabilized. I saw him just a couple of weeks later and he thanked me for being there and told me that he felt 100% better. He told me the plans he had to hold himself accountable and to make sure he was making good decisions. I gave the glory to God and shared hope in a relationship with God.

He not only agreed but prayed with me to make sure that His relationship with Jesus was established and growing.

Mike's story does not end there. He began his new life of hope as we visited each week for encouragement and some scripture to share. I was reassigned to another company after about a year and Mike was doing well, established, healthy and walking with our Lord. I am convinced more than ever that having any chance of keeping someone from hurting themselves begins with us and the relationships we have with each other. This world is nothing but trouble. Jesus said in John 16:33 ESV "I have said these things to you, that in me you may have peace. In the world you will have tribulation. But take heart; I have overcome the world." That is a good thing.

Here are a few tips for when you encounter someone who needs your help:

Get to know professionals who have experience dealing with depression and suicide prevention. Maybe a counselor or pastor or a professional who can circumvent any situation. You just never know when you will be confronted with someone who needs your help. Getting to a medical professional right away would be the best scenario.

The main thing to do is to make sure the person is safe. You do that by asking the affected person questions and then make sure you do not leave them alone unless you are sure they will not hurt themselves or anyone else for that matter.

Some of the questions you may ask are: What are you thinking right now? You are surely acting down and that is not like you. What is bothering you? You want to get them to talk. They will most likely speak to someone they trust.

I want to know that the person who said they were going to hurt themselves has no way of making that happen. Is there a gun? Where is it? How will they get it into their hands? Just ask questions that will alleviate any danger.

Next, get them to a medical professional who can ascertain what to do next and how to treat the mental, physical, and psychological aspects.

Thinking about suicide and having a plan to carry it out can be two different things. Can be, but not necessarily. When we have depressing thoughts, we must do something with them. The deeper we get with the depressing thoughts, the more dangerous and stifling they become. There are some vital steps for a Christian believer to take that will help them. The following steps must be practiced.

Limit Your Time on Social Media

We can all agree that this world can be depressing. Many times, I hear people repeat what social media is reporting, and what the talk radio station or the television is screaming. As a minister, I must not get so involved in the media as to skew my attitude, good or bad, and pass that on to the people I minister to. I am thinking of the political climate, as an example. Even if I love President Trump, I certainly must be careful how I say it to others because my desire is to reach others for our Lord. Putting down one person to bring up another will not be an effective way to minister to people with opposite political views.

My point for a believer is that we must get into the Bible and learn from our King, not social zealots that will hear nothing but their own opinions. Opinions are like intestines, everyone has them. Some of them, we just cannot stomach.

Surround yourself with people who will encourage you often; people who realize that we have no control over what other people do or say. We only have control over decisions we make and the actions we practice.

Get Your Eyes off Yourself

This is probably one of the most effective ways I deal with life when I am a bit down in the dumps. It's a great remedy, most of the time. We must get our eyes off ourselves. We have opportunities to reach out to people we know. There is always someone who could use an encouraging word or action to lift them up. We really do not know when people are down until we ask or even just reach out to them. Many times, we could say something like, "I was just thinking about you" or "Can I give you a call sometime just to hear how you are?" Make sure you call! Most of the time, the phone call of encouragement will be right on time. It is another Work of the Heart. Many times, I would hear, "I needed that phone call." You will be amazed at how timely a phone call or a word of affirmation can affect another life.

Be the encourager, even when you are not encouraged. You are giving of yourself to someone who needs to hear a good word. Here are encouraging words from Dr. Luke: Luke 6:38 (NLT) "Give, and you will receive. Your gift will return to you in full, pressed down, shaken together to make room for more, running over, and poured into your lap. The amount you give will determine the amount you get back."

CHAPTER FIVE

THE SPIRIT OF THE HEART

Just as God created you to do great things, He has created others in the same way. Choose to see God's action with the folks you interact with daily.

Faith at Work

I was in the job of my dreams. How much better could it be than going into workplaces and getting to know the people in the whole company on a personal level? Interacting with the owner or president of a company, to the person on the forklift loading trucks, what a perfect fit! Each week, I would go through all levels of the company, getting to know the people who work in each office, building relationships that will last a lifetime. I was excited to do this work of God. I encouraged people to be the best they could be for their families, their careers, and their future. I had a sense of awe that God would even think of putting me in this place at this time. I was incredibly grateful.

Have you ever just stopped and thought about what is going on in your life? What God is doing, how He is growing you personally, and how He is using you to minister to other people? I hope this next story excites you into a realization that God will use you right where you are, to reach people with hope, right where they are, despite your attitude! Let me explain...

A Heart Mechanic

I worked with a national ministry called Corporate Chaplains of America for fifteen years. This story started the first three months of my work as a Chaplain. We had an account at a local car dealership to care for their people. The company had a sales department, a body shop, various administrative offices, and a good size mechanic shop with about thirty mechanics. One morning, I was in the parts department speaking with the manager when a mechanic came in to pick up some parts. Pete had been a mechanic for many years. Each time I visited, he would be pleasant, but always busy with something. When Pete saw me, he asked if I would stop by his bay and talk for a minute. I acknowledged him and told him I would be with him after seeing the folks in the parts department.

At this point, I had been visiting the company for about three months, once or twice a week. This was my very first company and the very first car dealership for Corporate Chaplains of America. I wanted to do a great job, but my work did not seem to be as effective as I hoped. People were friendly and all, but I had not shared the gospel as often as I thought I would. I was building good relationships, but my expectations were not realized.

So, I made my way back to see Pete. He was working on a car that was on a lift while talking to me. That was usually how it worked. He would talk to me while working on something else, rarely looking me in the eye. He was always moving around. Pete and I had a decent relationship; pleasant, joking, and getting to know each other after only a few months as the Company Chaplain. I was able to get him to tell me about his wife and kids and a little about his background being raised in North Carolina. He was very personable at times but a bit tentative to share at a deeper level after only knowing me for a short time. He told me he grew up going to church with his family. Pete had a stable upbringing and a strong family. I was getting to know him quite well.

Picture this: he is working on the car and he begins to tell me how his wife is going to church and talking to him about going himself and this has been causing some arguments in the house. "So, what do I do?" he asked! I asked Him what he wanted me to do about his wife going to church and him not. He told me that I was the Chaplain and that I should be able to tell him what to do. I immediately did something I had never done up to that point.

Do You Allow God to Take the Reins?

I asked him to look at me and stop what he was doing. I then proceeded to kind of chew him out. I asked him if he really wanted me to tell him what to do. He said yes, so I proceeded to tell him what to do. Keep in mind that I am already not seeing fruit in the company and I am a bit frustrated. I said something like this: "Step up and be a man of the house. Step up and lead your wife and kids on a spiritual level." I told him that his wife was hungry for leadership. She is searching for spiritual direction that she is not getting from her husband. He just stood there while I continued. I then took out a little booklet I carried in my shirt pocket. It clearly outlined the Gospel of Jesus Christ. By this time, the rest of the mechanics were listening to our conversation. I did not realize just how loud I was. The New York attitude was out for all to see and hear.

I shared with him the good news but not exactly how I expected to share it. I was straight to the point and Pete seemed like he was paying attention. Amazingly he looked at me the whole time I spoke to him. He asked a couple of questions, but nothing about the gospel. So, I ended the conversation by handing him the gospel booklet with a clear presentation of what the Bible tells us about our relationship with God and how to make decisions going forward. He put it in his pocket. I told him that the booklet contained what I just told him for the most part and I asked him to take it home and read it when he had a chance. Then I said, "How about some lunch tomorrow?" He agreed with meeting for lunch tomorrow, and we went our separate ways.

The next day, I showed up at the shop about noon for our lunch date. Pete informed me that he had to go for a random urine analysis on his lunch break and couldn't make our meeting. Now my spiritual antennas were up. I was thinking that the devil does not want me to say anything more to Pete about Jesus, so He is stopping me. I know that is not healthy thinking, but it seemed as though God was using me to reach Pete. I was excited that I even had an opportunity to get him to listen and ask questions. My thought was that he trusted me enough to want to hear how he should handle his situation at the house with his family. God can easily bring Him into a real relationship with Himself, while bringing some light into his marriage. Pete said that he will be able to meet the next day for lunch, so off we went.

The next day, Pete and I met at the shop to go to lunch. Things were going smoothly. We exchanged pleasantries about work and the day as we traveled to the restaurant. There was something different in his demeanor that I could not put my finger on. He was relaxed and was kind of friendly in a different way. I was thinking he had a good conversation with his wife and things were looking up for him.

We arrived at the restaurant and Pete sat opposite me. Within the first couple of minutes, he had a smile on his face. What he said next blew my mind. He told me that he read that little booklet I gave him a couple of days ago and came to the realization that he needed to have a personal relationship with God. He told me that he prayed for Jesus to begin a good work in his heart and help guide him to lead his family in a spiritual sense. He wanted to lead his wife and he promised God to act on his decision. The smile turned into tears. I had no words to say at that moment except I thought it was the best decision he will ever make. Beginning that day, Pete and I grew together in our Lord. I was able to help him understand how to get the most out of his Bible. I would give him some direction on how to pray and what to expect in the days ahead.

After my lunch meeting with Pete, I found myself sitting in my car weeping uncontrollably. With tears in my eyes, I rejoiced over Pete's life transformation and what that would mean for the future of his family. I knew that God would work great things in their lives.

The Spirit worked His wonders in a way that I would never have imagined. Proving once again we cannot stop the work of God. I had a personal attitude towards Pete. I was frustrated in the way he communicated with me without eye contact. I blamed my abrupt demeanor on my New York way of talking. I have not spoken to anyone in that tone of voice since that day. I marked that day as the beginning of a significant ministry that would influence my attitude and submission to the Holy Spirit of God. I will never forget the first person I saw come to a personal relationship with Jesus Christ, despite me!

I had to surrender and let go of my attitude to really show up for Pete and allow God to work through me. I took the relationship I had with Pete personally and I did not appreciate the way he spoke to me. I had to realize that despite my own persona, God will work in any situation. He used me and taught me lessons about Him that I needed to know for future growth.

Be Persistent, but Not a Pain

Building relationships with people takes time and patience. They must receive your personality and trust you before a strong relationship can be realized. Being patient, surrendering to God, and allowing Him to work through you is the most important aspect of building relationships with people.

Ready to Share Hope for the Heart

The workplace is a place where relationships are built. We spend hundreds of hours with people outside our immediate families. God will use you in big ways when you realize how valuable you are to Him. There are practical steps you can take to effectively help people at work through life issues with a strong relationship with God.

Step 1 – **Be Spirit Sensitive**
An intimate relationship with God always begins with prayer. Prayer is a conversation with a friend that you know and desire to get to know deeper. Your heart must be softened. Prejudices have no place or purpose.

Pray often – Prayer must be part of who you are. The Bible says in 1 Thessalonians 5:16-18 (NLT) to "Always be joyful, never stop praying, be thankful in all circumstances, for this is God's will for you who belong to Christ Jesus." This is not a picture of a monk repeating prayers all day long. It is a picture of a relationship that is continuous and conscious. God knows our hearts, the who, when, and where we are always. He is gracious and merciful at each step.

Study the Bible - The most effective way to grow spiritually is to know your Bible. The Bible says of itself in Hebrews 4:12 (ESV) "for the Word of God is living and active, sharper than any two-edged sword, piercing to the division of soul and of spirit, of joints and of marrow, and discerning the thoughts and intentions of the heart." Read that again.

Associate with people of Faith – Surround yourself with like-minded people that will encourage you in faith. Hebrews 10:12 (NLT) "And let us not neglect our meeting together, as some people do, but encourage one another, especially now that the day of his return is drawing near." Yes, that can be the church building on a Sunday morning or social interaction during the week. The objective is to encourage one another in the Lord. You will read more about church in a later chapter. I believe that the gathering of people on a Sunday morning is likened to a hospital where we all come to strengthen one another.

Listen to the Spirit – John 15:26 (NLT) "But I will send you the Advocate—the Spirit of truth. He will come to you from the Father and will testify all about me."

Step 2 - **Be Prepared**
Be ready to share the Gospel – The gospel means good news. Everyone wants to hear good news, especially during times of bad news. At the time of this writing, the world is being affected by a virus pandemic. We need good news. What better time to share the gospel's good news with everyone you know.

Be ready to share your testimony - 1 Peter 3:15 (ESV) "put in your hearts honor Christ the Lord as holy, always being prepared to make a defense to anyone who asks you for a reason for the hope that is in you; yet do it with gentleness and respect."

Be ready to share a word for someone - Always have a word of encouragement for everyone you meet. Scripture covers every single issue we have in life, know what it says.

Step 3 - **Be Patient**

Be mindful – The key here is to realize what little control we have in life. Yes, we control what we say most of the time and how we react to any given situation, unless you are out of control.

Be focused on serving – This makes all the difference when we do what the Bible says towards other people: Philippians 2:3 (ASV) "Do nothing from selfish ambition or conceit, but in humility count others more significant than yourselves." Another important verse is Matthew 20:28 (NLT) "For even the Son of Man came not to be served but to serve others and to give his life as a ransom for many."

Be committed to people – People are here for us to serve. When we make a commitment to do just that, we will experience the joy that our Lord intended.

PART TWO
THE TOOLS OF FAITH

CHAPTER SIX

REFLECTIONS OF THE HEART

Who Am I? That is a powerful question to ask and to answer properly. You are made by God for God. And when you integrate God's identity for you into your heart and life, you will do mighty works with God.

Your God-Given Identity

There is a big difference in how we see ourselves and how God sees us. Many of us do not realize the difference unless we take the time to know what the Bible says. For example, take the word of an adult who verbally abuses a child in the early years of life. Speaking to a child as worthless will harm them for a lifetime. The damage is extremely dangerous and certainly not productive for the child's future. Can that kind of talk be the way that person identifies who they are? Sure, it can. Is it true? Of course not but hurt goes from one person to another.

Verbal and Physical Abuse Lasts a Lifetime

At this point, let me define the differences in verbal and physical abuse. Verbal abuse may not be realized until later in life. Many times, the abusers are not even aware that their words or attitudes are abusive. The abusers may have been victims themselves. Unfortunately, many parents do not take time to evaluate how they speak with their children. Good and bad words last a lifetime. It can be a struggle to learn this lesson.

We hear much more about physical abuse than we do verbal abuse. Many times, verbal abuse is more damaging than physical abuse. They both affect the mental stability of the abused, but harsh words seem to infiltrate the whole person with more subtle damage. The damage can last a lifetime in both cases. My experience is limited to the twenty years I have been interacting with people in ministry, but the experience has proven educational in each case. The point is that any abuse, whether physical or verbal, has a long-term effect on the abused person. You may have experienced abuse growing up as a child and know how it affected you as an adult.

Growing up in the city of New York with a broken family had its ups and downs, but we were not abused. We knew what was right and wrong and usually paid the price with a bit of a "woopin" as they say in the South, or an "ass kicking" in the North. Even though my mother and father lived in a different part of the city, I knew they loved me. They told me often. Life went on and I grew up a bit and went into the Air Force at eighteen years old.

I introduced my wife Janice in a previous chapter. We met during our first year in the Air Force at our first assignment. She is a native Virginian. She was raised on a small farm with seven brothers and three sisters: eleven kids total. Her mom and dad were married the whole time living in the same house. The more I spoke to Janice, the more I fell in love with her. I asked her to marry me in 1979, and we were married in 1980. She was the opposite of me in many respects. I had (and still have) a big mouth and a very extroverted personality (though she has tempered me over the years). She is introverted with a quiet demeanor.

Over time as our relationship developed, I had no idea how her background would affect our marriage. Many couples are blind to the past until the past comes into play in the relationship. How do we handle stuff we have no idea about while learning about each other?

This is the sad part. My wife was not physically abused by her parents. She worked awfully hard on the farm from day to night, before and after school, but that was what you do on a farm. Most of the eleven siblings played their part in helping grow the crops. Janice played a big part, being a middle child. She was and still is not afraid to work hard. Her parents expected her to not complain, do what she was told, and then, she got a cookie.

One thing her parents left out that later proved to be vital to a strong self-awareness and confidence was telling her that they loved her. She never heard it. She would get up in the morning and work, then go to school, then work some more until she could go in the house. She cannot remember her parents ever saying they loved her.

Hidden Heart of Emotional Abuse

Several years into our marriage, she told me that there was a time when she considered killing herself because of the relationship she had with her parents. To this day, after forty-one years of a marriage, I can bring up some subjects that will invoke emotions of deep hurt. The reason I am mentioning this is to highlight what I believe to be emotional abuse. If you never tell your children, you love them or show concern for them, that is emotional abuse. It can be even more devastating than physical abuse. At least with a good woopin you know where you stand.

The way she was brought up gave her an identity, and that was who she thought she was, a hard-working woman that just went through life in a tenacious way. Her identity was whatever everyone thought about her. Here enters me, another insecure clown that thought a sense of humor would get me through life. She had no idea about what she was in for when she married me. I was a self-absorbed boy who was learning just how broken he was. One thing we had going for each other was that we thought we loved each other and told each other so all the time. Our identities were changing into what we thought of one another and what we learned about each other. I did not have a clue how to give my wife the love she missed as a child. There was a void that would take years to begin to fill, even continuing to this day. How does one insecure, broken person help another insecure, broken person? By identifying with one another, right? How did you grow up and how did your upbringing affect you now?

The story above is just one of many real-life stories about who we think we are with the self-identification we have developed over the years. You will be amazed what God can do if we realize and understand our identification through the eyes of our Heavenly Father.

Your identity is formed at a young age and is affected throughout your life journey. The troubles you have, the people you meet, and the situations you encounter can change the course of your life. You may be in a job that fits you perfectly or you may seem stuck in a position that you struggle in for years. Your identity impacts every area of your life.

The relationships you have developed over the years from childhood through teenage years and on to adulthood have formed your image of who you are, while contributing to the way you see yourself. A good self-evaluation on how others may see you can be helpful from time to time. Getting feedback from a spouse or a friend will help the journey.

How do you see yourself? Is it helping you mature? What you believe about yourself will determine your future possibilities. That is your self-esteem.

Your feelings and mood have an enormous impact on your life. I can safely say that feelings are circumstantial most of the time. Feelings can be tricky, seeming like they are always a reality in life. They tend to change with the tides. You certainly cannot rely on a mood to make you happy. Your mood can even deter you from making wise decisions. Moods can depend on how strong the sun is for that day or the possibilities of a rainstorm. You get my point!

How the World Can Influence Your Identity

We all know that the world we live in is not exactly where you want to hang out for any extended periods of time. Just look at the political climate and tell me that we can learn or understand how to love and care for each other. Then go to your Hollywood favorites and use them as role models. I do believe that we have several celebrities that love as God loves, but that testimony is drowned out by the social media of depressing tactics. There is nothing good about trusting your identity in how many likes you have on a Facebook post. Social media will destroy your identity every time. There will always be people that have nothing good to say about you or what you do or about anything for that matter.

Get excited about what God says about you. These Seven Pillars to a healthy self-image will help:

The Seven Pillars of Your God-Given Identity

Pillar 1 – <u>GOD'S IMAGE CREATED</u>
I created you in my image.

> *Genesis 5:1- (NKJV) "This is the book of the genealogy of Adam. In the day that God created man, He made him in the likeness of God."*

What God says – This is exactly the way I want man to be formed, exactly like I desire. So that I can show you clearly that I loved you from the beginning so much to make you in my exact image.

What this means to you – God does not make junk. You have a purpose and God wants you to look at it and to work it out His way.

Pillar 2 – <u>LOVING GOD</u>
I created you to love Me, says the Lord.

> *1 Cor 8:3 (NLT) "But the person who loves God is the one whom God recognizes."*

What God says – I am going to send you someone to show you how much I love you, Jesus Christ.

What this means to you – He gave us a will to love Him back the same way, trusting Jesus as our personal Lord. (This is where we get the power to love like He intended.)

Pillar 3 – <u>GOD'S PROSPERITY</u>
God plans for us to prosper in every way.

Prov 13:31 (NAS) – "Adversity pursues sinners, but the righteous will be rewarded with prosperity." Prosperity is not always about the money. We prosper in relationships, influence, education and so many more avenues.

What God says – He will not take away your will. You will have choices; however, obedience to His Spirit is essential to prosper in every way.

What this means to you – God will engineer a fulfilling life as your relationship with Jesus develops and He will never forsake you as you move through the challenges of life.

Pillar 4 – GOD'S LIFE TO DO AS HE PLEASES
God gives life and takes it away.

1 John 5:12 – (NAS) "Whoever has the Son has **life***; whoever does not have the Son of God does not have* **life***."*

What God says – I sent you Jesus for you to accept my love. If you reject Him, I cannot save you.

What this means to you – Determine where you are with God and accept His gift of Jesus for your life, now and eternally. A child of God will experience an abundant life.

Pillar 5- GOD'S UNCONDITIONAL LOVE
God's love for you is unmatched.

PSALM 136:2 –(NLT) "Give thanks to the God of gods. His faithful love endures forever".

What God says – For God so loved us like crazy, despite our rebellion, that He sent His Son for the imperative means of saving us, from ourselves now and to live eternally with Him. For life here on earth and forever in His presence. (Toner's impaired interpretation.)

What this means to you – Accept the source of Unconditional Love. Jude 1:21 "Keep yourselves in the love of God, waiting anxiously for the mercy of our Lord Jesus Christ to eternal life."

Pillar 6 – GOD'S WITNESS
God wants you to share what He is doing in you.

Once God gets a good hold on your heart, He changes your life. Your perspective of value, humility, and focus seeks to honor your Creator. These insightful words are worth repeating: "Our faith becomes stronger as we express it; a growing faith is a sharing faith." — Billy Graham

This is the most practical verse on sharing God's work in you: 1 Peter 3:15-16 (NIV) "But in your hearts revere Christ as Lord. Always be prepared to give an answer to everyone who asks you to give the reason for the hope that you have. But do this with gentleness and respect, keeping a clear conscience, so that those who speak maliciously against your good behavior in Christ may be ashamed of their slander."

What God says – The scripture in the last paragraph says all that must be said about sharing our faith. Sharing what God is doing in you is not an option. Get excited about the life you have in Him; The Spirit of the Living God indwells believers.

What this means to you – You will experience the fruits of the Spirit in your life, and they will be evident to others. People will respond when His Word is spoken.

Pillar 7 – GOD'S GLORY
God wants you to give Him the glory.

The easy part is taking the credit or glory for good things that happen. We are instruments that God cherishes. We are to be separate from the world. That means not to get caught up in the worldly solutions for relationships, money, politics, or any other subject that can be put as a priority before your Lord.

Phil 2:11 (NAS) "and that every tongue will confess that Jesus Christ is Lord, to the glory of God the Father."

What God says – Allow me to use you as an ambassador for my kingdom. Tell of the privileges of giving The Glory away from the Glory Giver.

What this means to you- You represent God in life. How is that working so far? Are you growing in your faith? Are you seeing God work in your family, your work, your social interaction with others? Get real with God and be honest with yourself if your relationship with Him is as you would like. If not, do something about it and get moving. His character is full of grace and action packed with mercy.

How to Use Your Christian Identity

The Seven Pillars above need attention and practice in every area of life. They have the principles that promise to give us the experience of an abundant life.

In your day-to-day life, be more cognizant or discerning while you are outside your home, whether at work or in a church family.

Make sure that your spouse understands and practices biblical principles through God's Word. Talk about the scripture often.

Most of us have built strong relationships at the place where we work for a paycheck. You have an opportunity to strengthen the people you get to know. Your faith at work can be a tool to minister to people right where they are in life. If you were called to work at one job, I can assure you, you are there to share how God got you there in the first place. Tell your story.

If I went into your workplace tomorrow morning and asked a co-worker if they knew you were a Christian, what would they say? How can you bring your Lord into the workplace?

Understand who you are as a Christian and how God sees you at work. Bring a caring, attractive personality everywhere you go. Be real. Pay attention to everyone you meet or even pass in the hall or office. Everyone at work has a story. God wants to love the people you speak with daily. Go to 1 Peter 3:15-16. Give an answer to the hope that lies within you.

Really understand that God has created no accidents, and you are at work for a purpose; to honor God so people will see the results of your relationship with Jesus Christ. Look at people and get to know people like you are, a broken vessel, that needs a physician. The only way you can show love is to care about those you work close to often. Because you care. Do you Care? Are you working out your faith at work? If not, then consider...

How to Strengthen Your Christian Identity

How can you take this tool of Christian Identity and make it so strong that it becomes a habit within you? You strengthen it in three ways.

First, you learn from the Bible who God said you are. Know that you have a purpose that He will fulfill in you if you let Him.

Next, Prayer. This will be hard at first because we are used to talking to someone that will speak right back to us in an audible voice. God may do that, but most likely, it will be in a still soft voice in the quietness of the time with you.

Finally, submit and obey His Spirit. He has placed in front of you - relationships, work environments and other people that need help knowing Him through you. You are just practicing your faith in a practical way that honors your God.

There will certainly be challenges along the way as you begin the adventure. Trust is going to be your biggest asset. You will have to trust God with your whole being then people will have to trust you. Having the credibility of a person true to His word will go a long way. In John 14:6 Jesus did say that "He was the Way, the Truth, and the Life, no one comes to the father but through Him."

When you become strong with the tools mentioned above, a new life will open for you. When you know how your personal Lord feels about you, His confidence will shine through you and folks will see the peace that they want to know. When that happens, God will continue to grow you as a representation of His mercy and grace.

CHAPTER SEVEN

THE GOD OF THE HEART

What is the gospel and why should it matter to you? The gospel is simply "Good News." That is what it means, literally. But it is much more than that. Good news is a rarity in today's world. The mainstream news networks rarely report good news. Mr. Rogers' neighborhood is no longer a part of American society. That is too bad! We need Mr. Rogers again. We wonder why people are getting more depressed. They hear only bad news! Good news is a message we want people to hear to be encouraged. When the news of the full gospel is proclaimed, it allows God to relay His promises. When a person receives good news, they can either believe the news or not. Many people are inundated with bad news for years, then they hear the good news of the gospel and reject it. There are others who hear the good news of God and accept His message and begin to grow in a strong relationship with Him as their Lord.

The gospel is intended to impact your relationships, your self-esteem, and your disposition. There are ways to use the gospel as a tool in these three areas of your life. The gospel is a heart change.

The World We Live in and The Gospel

What does the gospel look like and how can we prepare our hearts to share its message of hope and reconciliation? Reconciliation means to bring together opposing sides, to reconcile together and begin a new relationship. The Good news in the Bible is that God sent His Son Jesus for us, to reconcile with Him. He was the epitome of reconciliation. He came to earth as fully God and fully man. His main purpose was to reconcile and bring together sinful man into a pure righteous relationship with God, through Jesus. Jesus is the object of the good news. He is the source of the new relationship.

A cursory understanding of the two opposing sides must be clarified. Good news is only as good as we think it is. We must recognize it as good, but only after we understand the bad condition, we are in. If you believe you are OK and you do not need help with life, then the good news will pass you by time after time. How many times have you heard the good news of Jesus Christ and ignored it? The ignoring is a result of our own self-righteousness in which the Bible says that there is no one good. He came to save us from the sin that entangles us. Psalm 14:3 (NKJ) "They have all turned aside, they have together become corrupt; *There is* none who does good, No, not one." Let your heart embrace the tools of faith.

Tool 1 – <u>**I MAY NEED YOUR HELP**</u>

First, recognize that you need help navigating this life. We try to do life by ourselves and the results usually leave us wanting. The Bible talks about this as sin. Sin means that we have missed the mark. Picture a target far away with the bull's eye as the perfect shot, a long way off and almost impossible to hit. The key to understanding this is to understand that we all sin. We all miss the mark of perfection. We miss it daily. Admit it and say you are sorry; you did not know any better. God promises to forgive your sins, past, present, and future.

> *Romans 3:23 (NLT) "For everyone has sinned; we all fall short of God's glorious standard." Rom 3:12 (NLT) reads: "All have turned away; all have become useless. No one does good, not a single one."*

God says that no one escapes a sinful life. Sin began in the days of Adam and Eve and continues to infect each person alive. Now that is a virus! The Corona virus has nothing on sin. Everyone is sick from sin whether we recognize it or not.

This will help you understand that everyone is in the same boat with a need for a Savior. The more we understand our condition, the more we will understand others.

Tool 2 – <u>**KEEP YOUR SELF-WILL, IF YOU WANT**</u>

We all have a will; no robots allowed. We make choices that we have to live with for the rest of our lives. Choices that we make are either in line with God's way or they are not.

Proverbs 14:12 (NLT) "There is a path before each person that seems right, but it ends in death. The wages of sin is separation from God. God hates sin!"

God tells us: See your ways as contrary to my ways and be willing to turn from your ways and follow me. You can make the choice to follow me or go your way. God will never twist your arm or manipulate you into a relationship with Him. You can choose when and where to follow Jesus as your Lord. The sooner that happens, the more abundant your life will become on earth. Eternity would be something to look forward to when you leave earth. We'll all be leaving sooner or later.

John 10:10 (NAS) The thief comes only to steal and kill and destroy; I came so that they would have life and have it abundantly."

This is great news. You can choose to say yes to a life with Jesus. It will not be perfect because we are not perfect, but His Spirit will lead you in righteousness. The imperfections of the flesh do not go away until heaven! If you expect to make right choices all the time, you have a wrong view of the Gospel. We are assured that The Word of the Lord is true. Jesus tells the Apostle Paul in 2 Corinthians 12:9 (NLT) "My grace is all you need. My power works best in weakness." We are weak in ourselves; pride will argue.

Tool 3 – **JESUS IS LORD**

Look to the Life of Jesus. Make Jesus your Savior and personal Lord. He loved you first. You cannot love without Him loving you first.

2 Tim 2:5 "For there is one God and one mediator between God and men, the man Jesus Christ."

God tells us in John 3:16 (NIV) that "God so loved the world that He gave his one and only Son, that whoever believes in him shall not perish but have eternal life." God valued you enough to come and rescue you to be with Him forever. In the meantime, He wants you to live a great life on earth until He does call you home for good.

Tool 4 - **THE SPIRIT IS ALIVE**

Accept Jesus into your life in your spirit. You have become a new creation. The Spirit of God is alive and well and He promises that you will be sealed with His Spirit for eternity. He will not let you go. All that stuff you may have heard and saw as a child comes to life in a relationship with a living and active God.

> *John 16:7 (NAS) "But I tell you the truth, it is to your advantage that I go away; for if I do not go away, the Helper will not come to you; but if I go, I will send Him to you."*

God says, you are His child, and your life is His. All he wanted you to do is accept the fact that He sent His Son. You recognized that and said Yes. Jesus dwells in you by His Spirit, God the Holy Spirit.

Revelation 3:20 (NIV) "here I am! I stand at the door and knock, if anyone hears my voice and opens the door, I will come in a door and eat with him and he with me." You are saved from eternal damnation. Or, let me make this a bit more inviting by saying, you are saved from eternal separation from God. You have another lease on life from God's perspective; a spiritual life that you have never had before.

Tool 5 – **LIVE OUT YOUR FAITH**

Live out your faith with other believers in the workplace and beyond. Begin to learn more about faith and relationships with God and other people. There will be some differences based on what God does in your heart. How we submit to His will determines the outcome.

> *2 Corinthians 5:7 (NAS) "for we walk by faith, not by sight."*
> *Galatians 2:20 (NLT) "My old self has been crucified with Christ. It is no longer I who live, but Christ lives in me. So, I live in this earthly body by trusting in the Son of God, who loved me and gave himself for me."*

God says, I will help you live out your faith to maturity. Allow me to direct your life with my Spirit. Submit to me. By living out your faith, it will get stronger, and you will see the fruit of your labor. God will really "bless your heart", as we say in the South. You will grow in the way to see the world through His eyes.

How to Live Out Your New Relationship with Jesus Christ

Think about how you are living your life. You have a new outlook, to bring glory to God. Be aware of people who are hurting. They are everywhere - your workplace, your church, your social environment.

Live out your relationship with Jesus with your spouse. This is easy. (Not really.) Eph 5:25 (NAS) "For husbands, this means love your wives, just as Christ loved the church." He gave up His life for her. Love means Sacrifice.

Eph 5:22 (NLT) "For wives, this means submit to your husbands as to the Lord." Here we have a leadership principle for husbands and wives. God designed the husband to lead His wife in spiritual maturity. I totally understand that may not be the case in some homes. The principles of sacrifice and love are always appropriate, no matter what the situation is. Your relationship with your spouse is the most important relationship you can have on this earth. A serious study of what, how, and to what extent you need to develop that relationship is written in the Bible. Study well, young grasshopper.

Many times, the workplace is the place where we spend most of our time. With the Corona virus, we are seeing many people begin a routine in the privacy of their homes. Working from home has its own challenges. We must use the technology we have to build our relationships in the workplace. Face to face is the best, but there are other ways that are not as intimate. I like to look people in the eye and tell them how much I care. The computer skews the eye contact. But that should not stop you. How can you use the gospel to bring God into your workplace?

Continue to learn what it is to be a Christian. Get serious about your study in the biblical principles of "What would Jesus do?"

As a person who contributes to your workplace, stand out as an excellent worker. Practice kindness and humility in all circumstances. As a leader you have a wonderful opportunity to always influence those around you.

Start with prayer each day before work. Be fully engaged at work, even outside your comfort zone. Show a different character by allowing God to use you, not only the work you do, but the way you interact with co-workers. You will be more like Jesus.

Watch what you say and how you say it. Because that is who you are as a believer, the stronger you get in your faith and understanding of your responsibilities as a child of God, the more effective you will be at loving people the way God designed them to be loved. Interact and go tell people who are spiritually minded. They should be ecstatic that someone has come to them in faith.

Show genuine care for the people you work with daily. Our relationship with the Lord is a personal relationship. It is never self-seeking.

Always look out for the welfare of co-workers. Work with excellence and personal responsibility. The only way that this is accomplished is if you purposely desire to build relationships with people at work. Most people will be friendly towards a friendly person. You cannot fake a friendly relationship. Just look at most of our politicians, we can see right through them from a distance. People recognize fake!

You build relationships because all people need relationships. God is working through you to use you to be there for people and introduce His peace to others.

Understand your responsibilities as an ambassador for Jesus Christ. You represent Him at every corner. You are an ambassador in the workplace. You represent God in your words and actions. What you do and say and how you do and say it will be put under a microscope in some cases. That is why it's important to understand those that do not have the same spirit that you do.

How do you share your faith with the folks at work without hitting them over the head with a big fat Bible? Good question. Here are a few answers. Get to know people personally, so they will trust you. Build a personal relationship with co-workers, especially those going through hard times, such as the times we are in.

You show your faith to folks at work because that is who you are, a child of God, loved by God for eternity. The Spirit in you is God's Spirit and that is a Spirit of love and care for other people. You will show that because of your growing relationship with God.

How to Strengthen the Gospel Within You

You strengthen the "Good News" in three ways:

Prayer - Understand that prayer is the undergirding of a heart that desires to know God intimately. Without prayer, we will just speak to ourselves or others. We take the distorted experiences of others and make that conversation our most valuable resource. Your conversation with yourself is usually distorted by your own experiences and attitude at the time of the conversation. Your conversation with God will be fruitful and calming to your soul.

Purposeful Study of the Scriptures – Get a good study Bible that you can read systematically. Get into the habit of reading a portion each day. A good idea is to start with the Book of John. This book gives a good picture of who Jesus was and what He did when he was on the earth.

Another tip: Every time before you open your Bible, pray something like this: "Lord I open Your Word with a hungry heart and a clear mind. Teach me Your ways while giving me direction for the day. I look forward to learning all I can about You and Your plans for my life. In the name of Jesus, I pray, Amen!"

Relationship and Interaction with Other Believers - Proverbs 27:17 (NLT) "As iron sharpens iron, so a friend sharpens a friend."

You will face some challenges as you begin. For reasons unknown to you, some people do not like the fact that you show your faith at work and speak about Jesus. There are many reasons why they dislike anything to do with Christianity or the name Jesus. Do not be surprised by the attitudes of some, even if you are treating people with kindness. There will be some folks that have a damaged history of faith or lack of faith because of ignorance.

When you get stronger in your faith, God will give you a discerning spirit and you will continue to develop an attitude of kindness and service. You will see people from a broken perspective and desire to help, even with your own brokenness. By embracing what Jesus did for you by living in the power of the Gospel, you will do mighty works with God.

CHAPTER EIGHT
THE SPIRITUAL PRACTICE OF THE HEART

There have been hundreds of books written about the Holy Spirit outside of the biblical text. The books cover all angles of study. I have been a student of the Bible for about twenty-five years and every time I go in the Bible, I find out something new. I knew nothing of the Holy Spirit growing up as a child in the Catholic church. I heard The Holy Spirit mentioned when I made the sign of the crucifix. I would hear the Holy Spirit mentioned in prayers with passages of scriptures read by the priests in the Mass. My knowledge of the Holy Spirit was minimal from an intellectual view.

I never owned a Bible, never studied the Holy Spirit until I accepted the fact that Jesus came to save me from sin. I do not claim to be a theologian, although I study theology. There is a particularly important aspect to The Holy Spirit that must be mentioned. Understanding the work of The Spirit is not natural. We cannot understand the Holiness of God and the work of His Spirit unless it is spiritually discerned. What I mean by spiritually discerned is that it takes a supernatural work of God for us to begin to understand God through His Spirit.

> *1 Corinthians 2:14 (NKJV) "But the natural man does not receive the things of the Spirit of God, for they are foolishness to him; nor can he know them, because they are spiritually discerned".*

If you had talked to me about The Holy Spirit before I was drawn near to God, I would have thought you were somewhat of a lunatic. When I came to the end of my own self-righteousness and accepted Jesus as my Savior, I had no idea what that meant. My faith had to grow. If my heart was right, then the head had to catch up. Many times, it is the other way around. People go to church all their lives and never really understand how God works. They have a head knowledge of God, but their hearts are far from Him.

I was fortunate to have someone who helped me understand what I should do next. His name was Omar Garcia, an education pastor at a local church in San Antonio, Texas. He gave me a Bible and told me to read it. He directed me to the Book of Psalms 1st chapter. This began a journey of understanding that I can now clearly write about in this book. Omar did not tell me to listen to him. He said, listen to God.

The Heart First, then the Mind

Before I read the Bible, I prepared my heart through prayer. I asked God to show me Himself in the 1st Psalm. It was practical and applicable to life as I saw it, through the eyes of God. It explained the differences in good and evil, a good start for me. My heart was prepared to learn from God. I began to understand that once I submitted my life to Jesus, His Spirit entered my life, and I could live for Him. If the Holy Spirit did not enter my life, I would have continued to do things my way, possibly trying to figure God out intellectually. That is what we do, we try and figure things out and come up with some sort of a solution. If it is not of God, then it is my solution. Frank Sinatra's song "I Did It My Way" would have continued to be my life's theme song. There are a couple of passages in the Bible that come to mind.

Romans 8:9 (NKJV) says "But you are not in the flesh but in the Spirit, if indeed the Spirit of God dwells in you. Now if anyone does not have the Spirit of Christ, he is not His." Wow, that nailed my conviction, as it should yours. The Spirit of the Living God is just as alive today as He was 2,000 years ago when He resurrected Jesus from the dead. My spiritual life began to flourish.

Just a reminder from a few paragraphs back... 1 Corinthians 2:14 (NKJV) reads, "But the natural man does not receive the things of the Spirit of God, for they are foolishness to Him; nor can he know them, because they are spiritually discerned." This passage tells us very clearly that we must submit to God right where we are and allow Him to change our soul intention. If you want to know God's will for your life, let Him know your desires. Ask Him to help you understand how to live a life pleasing to Him, only by His Spirit.

Gods Spirit is Alive and Well!

Who is the Holy Spirit? The explanation of the work of the Spirit must come from the Bible. If you would have told me that the Holy Spirit is a person, that would seem to me to contradict what a person is - a living, moving, breathing physical person that I can see. I just have a hard time thinking of a ghost that I cannot see. I grew up watching "Casper" the Friendly Ghost" for the last forty to fifty years. Casper has been a popular theme in motion pictures, videos, and story books throughout the world. Casper was a nice ghost that helped people see something different from what they were experiencing. He helped them in life. They feared him at first, then he spoke softly and kindly, and they began to like him. That is the only ghost I knew, and he wasn't holy.

It is utterly amazing that God saw fit to send His Son Jesus to die for us on the cross. Jesus was on earth for thirty-three years, then He was crucified, died, and was buried. He could have stopped there, but we still needed help with life. Knowing that our heavenly Father loved us was proven with the physical death of Jesus. Now what? He dies and He was the savior of the world. He forgives us by the blood that He shed. He was sent from the Father for us. You know the story; He rose again then showed Himself to the many people on at least ten different occasions, starting with the disciples. John 14:26 (ESV) "But the Helper, the Holy Spirit, whom the Father will send in my name, he will teach you all things and bring to your remembrance all that I have said to you."

The Holy Spirit is a person, the third person of the Godhead. There is one God in three persons – The Father as our Creator, The Son as our Redeemer, and the Spirit as our Sustainer. There is no natural explanation for the godhead, three persons in One God. "There is but **one** divine **nature**, but there are **three** distinct **personalities** possessing that unified set of infinite qualities." (Christian Courier- Wayne Jackson) The three persons are always working together.

The Father Creator- Think through this for a minute. God created us and gave us some commands that would keep us in fellowship with Him. We blew that and disobeyed His instruction in the garden of Eden. Generally, as mankind, we went our own way and have continued to go our own way from then on. We ignored the disciplines He set out for us to obey. He desired and created us to have a relationship with Him from the very beginning.

He never took away our will because that would make us His robots, in a sense. He could create everyone to obey Him, but that would not be by our volition. He would force us to comply without any thought from us. He gave us a mind to make decisions for Him.

The next step was because of our disobedience. He sent His Son to give us an opportunity to make up our minds to have a relationship with God. His Son was 100% God and 100% man. That was a perfect way for us to understand that He created us in His image to have a personal relationship with Him. God saying something like "Look, I brought you a Savior that is perfect. You are not. Listen to Him and have a perfect relationship with me by trusting my gift to you in Him. Please listen to me, there is not but seventy years, or eighty if you are blessed, to be around on the earth. Trust me." (Toner Commentary.)

Jesus as the Redeemer- His blood was the price he paid to get you back from the spiritually dead. Our disobedience separates us from God and Jesus was sent to buy you back, in a sense. You accept the gift of Jesus and you are His for eternity. If we do not use our mind to come to Him by faith, there is nothing else He can do. It is a decision that involves a heart change, while exercising the mind. We can choose to accept the gift to be with God forever or not.

The Sustainer, God the Holy Spirit- Jesus only lived on earth for thirty-three years. When Jesus was teaching before His crucifixion, He made a powerful promise that He kept to this day for those who follow His Word. In John 14:15-18 (NASV) He says, "If you love Me, you will keep My commandments. I will ask the Father, and He will give you another Helper, that He may be with you forever; that *is* the Spirit of truth, whom the world cannot receive, because it does not see Him or know Him, *but* you know Him because He abides with you and will be in you. I will not leave you as orphans; I will come to you."

That is God's promise. The Holy Spirit is alive and well today. Trust His Word today. He is real or else I could not write about Him. I am giving testimony to His work in me.

The Holy Spirit impacts your life in:

Relationships – Recognize that God has no accidents. The people in your life at home, in the workplace, or even in the social environment are divine appointments. Get to know them and keep your heart open to what God is doing during the relationship.

Self-esteem – Despite how we grew up, what our parents told us about life or the circumstances we are in or were in, God loves you right where you are, during trouble or during joy. The way He thinks of you is different from the way others think of you. If you are His child, then you inherit the privileges of a King. Really, I am a child of a King? Yes, that is what the Bible teaches. Does that make you think any differently of yourself or of life?

Feelings and Mood – Your spirit determines your mood many times in life. The communion you have with God the Spirit will set the mood. When feelings come on that are not good, you know that it is not what God would want. And you know by His Spirit he will be there to call upon.

How does The Holy Spirit Operate?

There are many ways that The Holy Spirit operates, and it is important to understand how you can be in tune and follow the Spirit.

Way 1 – WHO WE ARE IN CHRIST

Scripture – Romans 8:16 (NKJV) – "The Spirit Himself bears witness with our spirit that we are children of God."

God takes your willing spirit and helps you know who you are from His perspective. As your faith grows stronger, you understand more about Him creating you as His child. The Spirit convicts and confirms based on His Word, the Bible.

There is a sense of freedom and joy knowing that you inherited eternal life while enjoying abundant life here on earth. Think about this: you can read about His work in the Bible, that is amazing! This is what He reveals:

Way 2 – REVEALS TRUTH

John 16:13 (NKJV) "*But when He,* **the Spirit of truth,** *comes,* **He will guide you into all truth.** *He will not speak on his own; He will speak only what He hears, and He will tell you what is yet to come.*"

In today's world, truth is what you want it to be for you, whatever you feel fits your objective. First, that is a lie right from the beginning. Truth is established by God in His Son. Jesus said, "I am the way, the truth and the life, no one can come to the Father except through me". John 14:6 (NLT)

When you know Jesus, He will help you discern truth from a lie. The devil is the father of lies, John 8:44. You will know the difference when you understand and realize the truth.

If you know the Truth, you can tell a counterfeit. I learned something interesting: federal agents in the money counterfeiting department do not spend a whole bunch of time studying fake money. They study the real money. They know it like the back of their hands, so that if a fake bill comes in, they recognize the fake quickly. Sometimes, it takes a bit more time because it is a good lie. Eventually, the lie is exposed, and the truth is revealed. You know the Truth through the Spirit and you will spot a lie a mile away once The Holy Spirit is at work in you. Knowing truth makes life much more discerning.

Way 3 – HE IS A TEACHER

> *John 14:26 (NKJV) "But the Helper, the Holy Spirit, whom the Father will send in My name, will teach you all things and bring to your remembrance all things I said to you."*

You are a new creature. Your mindset is tuned to the Spirit of God. You will learn about Him and learn about your life and the lives of others according to His Word. You receive a clearer direction for life and a sense of purpose from knowing that you are a student of God.

Way 4 – MAKES US HOLY

> *1 Corinthians 6:11 "And that is what some of you were. But you were washed, you were sanctified, you were justified in the name of the Lord Jesus Christ and by the Spirit of God."*

Being sanctified is a church word meaning continuously coming closer to the Lord, growing in faith. Justified means to be made right. That happens when we accept the sacrifice of Jesus and become one in Him because of Him. We are made right!

He gives us a sense of separation from what the world is doing. That is a good thing in most cases, a different perspective that instills in us the desire to honor the Father in every aspect of life.

I have never thought of myself as holy. Have you? Far from being holy, I find myself in the opposite spectrum. Unholy and dirty in a sense. The Bible says that as believers, we are separated unto holiness. We are in Christ who is holy, so we are to be holy, separated from the world but in the world to show holiness through Him. We are being cleansed by the blood on a continuous basis and sanctified. (growing in faith)

Way 5 – HE BRINGS POWER

Acts 1:8 – "But you will receive power when the Holy Spirit comes on you; and you will be my witnesses in Jerusalem, and in all Judea and Samaria, and to the ends of the earth."

We desire to share what God is doing in our lives. His Spirit awakens our spirit. There is the power of conviction and restoration that people need, and we are compelled to tell others. We should show this in our daily lives and give out The Word of God to people.

We gain a new perspective about life, and our hearts are willing and able to share that perspective from God's viewpoint. He becomes experiential in you and He is honored.

Exercise the Heart of the Spirit

The Holy Spirit leads your life; you base all the decisions you need to make on your relation to His Spirit. He will guide us in all truth.

With your spouse, **He's First.** There is no other relationship more important on this earth than your relationship with your spouse. Allow God to lead you both in marriage. His way will bring eternal security in your marriage and joy in the relationship.

In your closest relationships at work, **He Works.** He works all the time. The many hours at work you will spend with others will give you an opportunity to live out your faith in front of them. The words we use and the actions we live show the work of God in your life. Allowing God's Spirit to lead, you will make your workplace more effective for you and your co-workers.

The Holy Spirit in the Workplace

Understand Your Responsibilities in the Workplace

Your job is important to the company. Being reliable, trustworthy, and valuable to the company will go a long way. Knowing God's plan for you at work will only enhance your experiences.

Be attractive to others by practicing excellent work ethics. There should be something different about you that people will want to know about. You set the example as a leader, people are watching you and desire to work with you more often.

You work with excellence because you honor God through your talents, abilities, and solid work ethics. His Spirit is evident through you.

<u>Understand Your Responsibilities in Your Relationships with Co-Workers</u>

You interact with co-workers in various situations. Each person you work with will see how you work and how you show your loyalty. Your actions speak louder than your words. Here is a good place to show people you are blessed. Let your light shine. Let excellence in what you do be the standard.

Honor God first and foremost. Others will see your good works. God gave you the abilities to honor Him.

<u>Be Consistent in All You Do</u>

Consistency is a key to a solid workplace experience. Keep in mind that faith is always worked out. Faith is practiced. When something is practiced, it becomes permanent, not perfect. Perfect faith is only lived through a perfect person. Jesus Christ was perfect, while we are on the earth in our flesh, our perfection can only be in Him.

It takes patience, prayer, and perseverance. If you are wrong, admit it and apologize right away.

People will realize you are a human being, but you have a mindset that may be different because You desire to be more like Jesus.

How to Be Strengthened by The Holy Spirit Within You

<u>Understand we are in a Spiritual Battle</u> that we cannot win alone. Learn what the Bible says about The Spirit and the weapons of warfare in Ephesians 6:10-14. We do not have to look far to see evil practiced in this world. Knowing that evil exists will help us begin to understand what a

believer is up against. A believer must be equipped with the full armor of God, in Ephesians 6.

Prayer will be essential in growing our faith. What prayer does is humble us to be able to look outside ourselves and allow God to teach us spiritual discernment inside.

Talk about your walk with the Lord with other people. Now, keep in mind when you speak about your relationship with God, there are responsibilities that come with your confession. Tell other people what God is doing.

The Challenge of the Heart

The biggest challenge you will have is the discipline of consistent study. Look for God's work through you in how you treat others and how you look at other people. Walking with the Spirit of God is a lifetime activity, starting with the realization that The Spirit indwells you and you can call on Him at any time. Your desire to grow closer to the Lord will increase and your action and feedback from others will be one of joy.

By integrating the Holy Spirit's work in you daily, you can bring God into all areas of your life. By tuning into, following, and being empowered by the Holy Spirit, you will do mighty works for God, with God.

CHAPTER NINE

GOD'S LOVE LETTER TO THE HEART

Did you have a Bible when you were growing up? Where was it in the house? On the Table? In a drawer? On the shelf collecting dust. Our house did not have a Bible. I grew up in an Irish-Catholic neighborhood in New York City. Honestly, I didn't know of anyone who owned a Bible. I'm not saying no one did, but I did not know any. I was an altar boy at the local Catholic church, so I saw a huge Bible on the altar. Only the priest would read from it. I don't remember them ever picking it up. It was too big to handle. I assume the priest had another one at their house that they read. The first Bible

I owned was when I came to the Lord at the age of thirty. That was given to me as a gift. I have not put it down since.

Here is something to ponder: Did you know that there are over 100 million Bibles sold or given away each year? Two and a half billion were printed in the last fifty years. That is "B" for billion, truly an amazing number. Here is a sad statistic according to Statista, only 3% of adults in the United States read their Bibles every day. About 35% have never read the Bible. In 2018, it was 16% that read it every day and we are down to 3% in 2020. Here is another interesting fact - 92% of households in the United States have at least one Bible in their house. If I were a betting man, I would say that the percentage of people having a Bible in the North East is considerably lower than the South.

Why don't people read the Word of God? Let us be honest, there is nothing attractive about the Bible. Most of them have a black cover with the word "Bible" on the front. Inside, we see chapters and verses and different titled books. It has no pictures, nothing to entertain. The only pictures may be maps in the back. We are in a time in history where people want to visually see results and glamour. They want to be entertained behind a computer with games, data, sensational movies, and the like. The Bible does not do that.

The Bible addresses every single issue in life, every issue! You have a marriage problem? It is in there. Money problem? It is in there. What about teenager issues? That is in there, too! There is not one issue that we deal with that is not addressed in the Bible. Why won't most people read the Bible if it addresses the issues we all experience? I have my own theory, but there are a few reasons that are not so obvious.

I spoke a little about Spiritual Warfare. If I were the devil, I would not want you to read the Bible. There might be a chance you would really learn the truth about God. It takes work to read the Bible. Most people do not read books like they have in the past, the computer is a lot easier to access.

Now, there are plenty of Bible resources on the internet. But there are also more distractions to keep you away from the Bible on the internet unless you go to The Word on purpose. That is the reason I suggest reading a printed hard copy in your quiet place.

The Bible says in Ephesians 6:10-12 (NLT) "Be strong in the Lord and in his mighty power. Put on all of God's armor so that you will be able to stand firm against all strategies of the devil. For we are not fighting against flesh-and-blood enemies, but against evil rulers and authorities of the unseen world, against mighty powers in this dark world, and against evil spirits in the heavenly places."

The Word of God is Powerful

Hebrews 4:12 (NLT) "For the Word of God is alive and powerful. It is sharper than the sharpest two-edged sword, cutting between soul and spirit, between joint and marrow. It exposes our innermost thoughts and desires."

The Word of God is Practical

It's practical for your life. Read what it says in 2 Tim 3:16-17 (NLT) "All Scripture is inspired by God and profitable for teaching, for reproof, for correction, for training in righteousness; so that the man of God may be adequate, equipped for every good work."

The relationship we have with all people will be enhanced because we know more about what God says about them and how we are to treat others. He gives us clear direction on people problems.

You will look through the eyes of God, not just the way you were raised. Your self-esteem is seen through the eyes of your Heavenly Father. Feelings most likely will be circumstantial, and mood will be in control. You will know what is perfect for the situation from what God says in His Word.

How does the world imitate the Word of God? Keep in mind that two of the top bestselling books of all time are "Little Red Book" by Mao Ze Dong, the leader of the Communist party, and the books from the Harry Potter series. Who does not have those for our kids to entertain? Harry is an English Wizard. These two books have sold hundreds of millions of copies throughout the world. Harry Potter especially has infiltrated millions of homes here in the US. Children are taught to read Harry Potter, but have no idea of the impact of what is in the books or what the Bible teaches about the content of the books. They can tell you all the names of the wizards but have no idea who Moses or even Adam is, never mind the prophet, Isaiah.

Did you know that the Bible condemns any sort of witchcraft? You may not know that unless you read the Bible. The Bible has much to say about the subject in 1 Samuel 15:23 (NKJV) "For rebellion is as the sin of witchcraft, and stubbornness is as iniquity and idolatry." Witchcraft is Satan's realm, and he excels in counterfeiting what God does.

I know that Harry Potter is a good friend to well-meaning moms and dads everywhere, whether they are Christians or not. Please do not be surprised if your children grow up riding broomsticks off tall buildings in a single bound. (Only joking, but not really.) Teaching our children principles laid out in the Word of God will give them an understanding of what is healthy for their future endeavors. You and they will know if Harry and Mao will direct their path in a healthy way.

You have heard it said that you are what you eat. It is true. Be hungry for the Word. Eat as much of it as you can. Get your fill, or this world will have its fill of you without you even realizing its implications. The prophet Jeremiah told us in his own words 15:16, "When I discovered your words, I devoured them. They are my joy and my heart's delight, for I bear your name, O LORD God of Heaven's Armies".

Here are some pillars of truth from the Word of God that you can stand on and trust in every day:

Pillar 1 – **The Bible is True - Without Error - every word**

Thessalonians 2:13 (ESV) "And we also thank God constantly for this, that when you received the word of God, which you heard from us, you accepted it not as the word of men but as what it really is, the word of God, which is at work in you believers."

The words in the Bible are alive. Trust them. If faith were not enough, which it is sufficient, we would find that all the good in the world is in the Word. The principles are practical and able to be practiced even naturally as humans. We may not even realize The Spirit at work. The Word is alive, whether we know it or not. Just look at the difference between good and evil. I trust good, do you?

Knowing the Word by faith in the Lord will open doors of wisdom and understanding for your life on earth and with Him for eternity.

Pillar 2 – **The Bible Teaches God's Direction**

Psalm 19:7 (ESV) "The law of the LORD is perfect, reviving the soul; the testimony of the LORD is sure, making wise the simple."

God's Word proves true every time. The reassurance that God will be true to His name and nature will give us a sense of peace that we cannot have in a relationship to man. Proverbs 3:4-5 (NKJV) tells us to "Trust in the Lord with all our heart and lean not on our own understanding and in all our ways acknowledge Him and He shall direct your path."

Pillar 3 – **The Bible Addresses All Life Issues**

2 Timothy 3:16-17 (ESV) "All Scripture is breathed out by God and profitable for teaching, for reproof, for correction, and for training in righteousness, that the man of God may be competent, equipped for every good work."

The best way to trust His Word for your life is to practice the principles outlined in the verse above. There is a sense of yielding that must take place. Humility is a vital connection between the words of God and your instinct to trust in what you know.

This can be the difference between a joyful life of security and one of constant search for significance and peace.

Pillar 4 – **The Bible Strengthens Your Spiritual Maturity**

John 17:17 (ESV) "Sanctify them in the truth; your word is truth."

To sanctify means to grow up spiritually. Maturing in faith will affect every aspect of life. Get stronger in your faith!

If we would just make a consistent effort to open our hearts to the Word of God and ask Him to grow us up in maturity for Him, about Him, we would experience life abundantly. I repeat the message of yielding to His Spirit.

A consistent search of scriptures will prove to be extremely beneficial for your faith journey and those around you will benefit from the wisdom gained through this exercise. Searching the scriptures does take discipline, but the work will be worth every minute.

Pillar 5 – **The Bible Changes Man's Heart Towards God and Man**

> *Hebrews 4:12 (ESV) "For the word of God is living and active, sharper than any two-edged sword, piercing to the division of soul and of spirit, of joints and of marrow, and discerning the thoughts and intentions of the heart."*

We can trust it because it is true and alive. The words come to life as we practice our faith. There certainly will be bumps along the way, but as we all know, trials make us stronger if we have the right attitude and understanding.

When our hearts are changed, we will see things differently. There will be opposition to a stronger walk-in faith. There will always be war when good and evil intersect. Spiritual warfare is real for a growing Christian and the Word of God not only assures victory but will teach us what to watch out for.

How to Use the Word of God

Begin with reading about the life of Jesus. He sets the example of how to live a life God's way. He practiced the principles God outlined in His Word. A good place to start is the gospel of John. Just read it through first, then a second time a little slower, thinking through the sections of scripture to get a deeper understanding. That will give you a good start on learning how Jesus interacted with people during His thirty-three years of life on Earth. This will then give you a foundation on how to live life in your relationships. Further study in other parts of the Bible will develop as you grow in faith.

If you are married, you will see Jesus transform the way you treat your spouse, respect and dignity will be enhanced. The foundation for a lifelong relationship will be established and cemented. Practicing the principles outlined in the book will strengthen your marriage, increasing knowledge on how God sees the marriage relationship, along with relationships outside of marriage.

The workplace is a place where we spend plenty of time building relationships. The relationships that you develop at work, by knowing what the Bible teaches, will bring transformation to those around you. God will bless your sphere of influence as a leader.

God's Word Establishes Trust at Work

You bring God into your workplace by going to work. When you have confessed that Jesus is your Lord, the Spirit of God lives inside you. Keep that in mind. You are to be an ambassador for Jesus, first and foremost.

As an ambassador, you are a representative of God. That is an awesome responsibility. The question is, do you want to develop that relationship and pass on the influence or not? That is up to you.

Listen well to your coworkers. You may share some scripture with those that need an encouraging word and hope for the future. Just a thought: Have a daily verse to keep in your mind and tell your closest co-workers what you learned.

Because you desire to be the best leader you can to influence others for God, He will use you in big ways.

Build Trust with people. The more you know people on a personal level, the more they will trust you. Probably the best way to build trust is not to ram Bible knowledge down the throats of coworkers. Live out your faith without creating a threat.

A big part of trust is always to be **confidential** with the conversations you have with people at work. Never tell anyone else about someone who trusts you or you will lose a coworker and friend forever. No Gossip.

You built trust so you will be the one people go to if they have something on their hearts. It may be something significant that they will only tell people they trust.

Be a servant to others. Show people your heart by being available for them anytime. Assist in any area at work that needs another person outside your own responsibility. Serving people is a big part of leadership. Having a servant attitude will do exactly what God desires you to do, to serve others.

Care about the people within your company and show that care through your words and actions. Lead by example as it shows your servant heart; your willingness to do whatever it takes to get the job done. It is great to be the go-to person for help when times are tough for others.

How to Strengthen the Word of God Within You

1. First, set up a systematic time when you will read the Bible each day. This takes discipline and direction. As I have said before, I recommend reading the Book of John first. The main reason I say that is that it gives you a good picture of Jesus and the ministry He had while on Earth. It will show His interaction with people and the way in which he loved them. He sets the example for us to follow.

Get a version of the Bible that you are comfortable reading. Some versions are a bit more difficult to read than others. The reason for that is the language interpretation. For example, the King James version is in Old English from the 1600's. Instead of "The" it may say "Thou" or "will" may be named like "wildst." They mean the same things, just in a different vernacular. I would recommend the New King James version which is a word for word accurate translation from the original Greek for the New Testament and the Original Hebrew from the Old Testament. There are other accurate translations that will read smoother. Here is a resource you may find helpful: www.biblestudytools.com

2. Set aside a time each day to be quiet before the Lord and read His Word. You can contact me personally if you have a question about where to start: www.heartsatwork.com.

3. Talk to another Christian about what you read. It is always a good idea to be plugged into a study with like-minded people. Age-appropriate Bible studies can be a good choice. If you have a spouse, join a couple's class where both of you are studying together.

You will face challenges as you begin. I can tell you without question that you will be opposed by spiritual warfare of the devil. If I were the devil, I would not want you to get closer to God, that is for sure. You must know that it is super easy NOT to read the Bible or take time to be quiet before the Lord. It takes work to grow in your faith. Please take the study seriously and make it a priority in life.

When you get stronger in your faith by reading the Word of God, you will see some tremendous changes take place. Your understanding of the work of the enemy will become clearer. You will be stronger for other people. You will be able to sharpen each other by encouraging each other to continue getting stronger. You will get spiritual wisdom to be able to handle all the circumstances you run into, good and bad. God will bless you beyond measure.

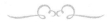

CHAPTER TEN
PRAYING FROM THE HEART

What is prayer and how can you use it as a tool of Christian leadership? No matter how much I write about prayer, it will not be sufficient to cover the subject. I guess I can get deep into the theology of a powerful prayer life. I have a prayer life, but at times I have no idea how powerful it is. Many times, I have intentions on spending more time in prayer, but get distracted as I would talking to a friend about a subject that interests me more.

There are a few things that I do know that are important when it comes to prayer. First, I have absolutely no control over what other people do. Second, I have no control over circumstances outside of my ability to give a reaction or take some action. Saying that, I understand that God is powerful. I know that by faith and the evidence of His creation. When

He changed my heart to follow Him and not trust my flesh, He also gave me a sense of hunger to develop a relationship with Him. Prayer is a relationship. It is a relationship that we have with a powerful God that desires us to relate to Him. It is up to us to be obedient to His Spirit in us.

Prayer is much more than a relationship. It is a heart's desire, an action step. Life is full of insecurity at times. This present age is a great example of our insecurities as a nation. Our nation is insecure, our people are insecure. Prayer is a divine relationship that must be initiated by me and you and powered only by the work of The Spirit. At first, it is a bit awkward, as with any new relationship. We must get to know the person at a deeper level, more than superficial. When I meet a new friend, I talk to them about superficial things at first, then after a while, I get deeper because I trust them more intimately. The depth of our relationship can either fizzle out or strengthen.

If you're married, you remember the first time you met your wife or husband? In the interaction, you may have delved into their childhood, certainly their interests, and maybe some of their dreams. If prayer is a relationship, then it only seems reasonable that your relationship is either developing or not. I will never get to know the one I love unless I get to know what they are thinking. I love my wife, so I desire to get to know her inner thoughts.

Of course, there are different types of relationships; Parental, sibling, friends, business associates and our relationship with God. The depth of the relationship is totally depending on your objective in that relationship. If I want to grow my marriage with my wife, she will have to be especially important to me, so I desire to get to know her. I cannot think of myself all the time because that will stifle the relationship.

If I have a business partner and I desire to grow our business, we will have to get deeper in the understanding of the business and how we both interact in the setting. Our relationship with God has remarkably similar principles on purpose. The biggest difference is that it starts with God all the time. We either obey His Spirit as a believer or disregard the relationship. Disregarding your relationship with God sets a rather dangerous precedence that I will explain.

Prayer should be practiced. When an athlete desires to get stronger for a competition, they work out continuously and consistently. They build muscle for the gold medal. They are competing not only with a formidable team or person, but they are also strengthening their confidence for the personal battle ahead. **Prayer practice makes permanence**. Prayer impacts your life by putting the focus on the object of your affection: Jesus Christ.

Every relationship is developed. It begins with two people and continues when the two people talk to each other. That conversation cannot be self-focused, it must be foundationally focused on the other person. First find out how the other person ticks, then learn how you tick regarding communion with the other person. That was a mouth full. Healthy communication is vital to any relationship.

Prayer as Healthy Communication

Humility is an especially important aspect of self-esteem. If we desire to learn from another person, we must listen to what they say intentionally open our heart to learning. The way we see ourselves is one thing, but the way God sees us is another. Unfortunately, many people believe what others say about them, even though it may be an outright lie.

I have said before that feelings are circumstantial. Truth be told, there are times when I do not feel like praying. Many of us get so wrapped up in what is happening around us, we do not even take time to rest, never mind talk to God. We are not in the mood! Prayer, like love, is not a mood thing. I am persuaded to love as God loves without condition. Prayer is similar; we are persuaded to talk to God as believers.

How does the world mock prayer? The natural world in which we live can only know about natural ways to communicate with each other. It comes to reason that anything from a supernatural relationship with a living God would not fit and would be looked upon as possibly something ludicrous and out of the norm. Read what the Bible says about people understanding spiritual things in 2 Corinthians 2:14 (NLT) "But people who aren't spiritual can't receive these truths from God's Spirit. It all sounds foolish to them and they can't understand it, for only those who are spiritual can understand what the Spirit means."

There are core pillars about prayer that will give you a powerful understanding of its practice and application in your life.

Pillar 1 – **Heart Change**

Prayer begins with Transformation of the heart. Look at this prayer from the Psalmist:

> *Psalm 10:17 (AMP) "O LORD, You have heard the desire of the humble and oppressed; You will strengthen their heart, You will incline Your ear to hear,"*

The heart works with the mind and your mind has been changed by The Spirit of God. You can trust God. He does not lie. His Word is true. His will be done. Your desire should be His will.

Pillar 2 – **Listening**

We all need practice in Listening. Most of us want to get our point across before we listen to others. Someone said that we are given two ears and one mouth so we can listen twice as much as we speak. It is important to prepare to listen before we engage in conversation. Our hearts must be ready to receive without prejudice and trust God for direction, for an engaging dialogue. Just listen to what is happening inside you. Effective prayer is not only words. Our amazing God wants us to just listen at times. Be still and enjoy the value of quietness.

Scripture reads, in Psalm 46:10 (NLT) "Be still and know that I am God! I will be honored by every nation. I will be honored throughout the world."

Try taking a minute right NOW and be quiet and listen. Close your eyes and be still, no distractions. It is music to the heart. Seems like it gets more difficult to stay still these days. Too many things going on at once. I am listening to soft instrumental music while I am writing this book. It helps my concentration of listening to God. Listening with an open heart is something like, "OK Lord, I'm ready for you to speak to me."

Praying calms the spirit. We experience peace and quiet away from the hustle of the world. Allow God to speak to you by taking the time to listen in a quiet place.

Pillar 3 – **Pray Scripture**

There are literally hundreds of prayers in the Bible. God gave the words to the writers to speak to Him. It is certainly appropriate for us to speak God's words back to Him from our heart. This is a remarkably effective way to pray. Give God's Word back to Him.

I suggest the book of Psalms. Psalm 63 (NLT) is wonderful. Pray this prayer now.

O God, you are my God;
    I earnestly search for you.

My soul thirsts for you;
    my whole body longs for you
in this parched and weary land
    where there is no water.
I have seen you in your sanctuary
    and gazed upon your power and glory.
Your unfailing love is better than life itself;
    how I praise you!
I will praise you as long as I live,
    lifting up my hands to you in prayer.
You satisfy me more than the richest feast.
    I will praise you with songs of joy.
I lie awake thinking of you,
    meditating on you through the night.
Because you are my helper,
    I sing for joy in the shadow of your wings.
I cling to you;
    your strong right hand holds me securely.
But those plotting to destroy me will come to ruin.
    They will go down into the depths of the earth.
They will die by the sword
    and become the food of jackals.
But the king will rejoice in God.
    All who swear to tell the truth will praise him,
    while liars will be silenced.

This prayer is attributed to King David as he traveled through the wilderness thirsty to hear from God. Are you thirsty to hear from God?

You can trust scripture because they are God's Words that he gave to us to dialogue with Him through His ordained authors. You will get to know God's heart by seeing, hearing, and saying His words to Him in prayers of your heart.

Pillar 4 – **Pray Always**

Live a life of Prayer. Prayer is part of who you are in Christ Jesus. It should be a natural part of a supernatural change in you. Sometimes we say second nature, but I am saying first nature. A changed nature of trusting in God's Spirit to lead.

1 Thessalonians 5:17 (NLT) "Never stop praying."

You know it takes strong, continuous communication to build a relationship, and this is the best way to build a relationship with God. Prayer communication is nothing more than a conversation with God about anything your heart desires. Talk to your friend that you love.

Let's be reasonable. This verse does not mean that we walk around talking to ourselves so that others think we're weird. What it does mean is that you have an ongoing relationship with God that is continuous and vibrant. You are speaking with Him all the time in your heart. You know He is listening to you as a father pays attention to a child while looking at each circumstance as building a stronger bond.

Pillar 5 – **Pray for Others**

This is called intercessory prayer, praying with and for other people.

Ephesians 6:18 (Amplified) "With all prayer and petition pray [with specific requests] at all times [on every occasion and in every season] in the Spirit, and with this in view, stay alert with all perseverance and petition [interceding in prayer] for all God's people."

We need the prayers of others. Pray for brothers and sisters in the Lord, the church, healing, financial concerns. I desire for you to pray for me, as I will for you. Prayer takes the focus away from us and shows concern for other people. It is also a testimony of God's work in you with others in mind.

How to Use Prayer

Prayer is a way of life for a believer, there can very easily be an emptiness if prayer is not practiced. Relationships, or lack of relationship communication, can be mighty lonely without a consistent prayer life.

If you desire to stay strong in your relationship with your spouse, then pray with them and for them. Pray for specific things, such as God's presence in the relationship, your family, your spiritual intimacy with the Lord and each other.

There are wonderful opportunities to intercede for specific people at work; and those that have specific needs. Prayer also builds trust if you are invited to pray with or for a coworker. Seek out believers and set up specific times when you can pray together.

Bring the Heart of Prayer to Work

There are many workplaces that encourage prayer at work under appropriate circumstances. Be the one that asks to pray at the start of an event, meeting, or special circumstance.

Identify Believers

Seek out other believers in prayer. Get permission from them to pray for them. Take the time to do just that. Pray for them or with them in a private place.

How do you pray at work? Get to know people at work and ask, invite, get permission so that it is not threatening. You are asking permission in all the circumstances.

Prayer builds the body of Christ. It strengthens the body. Matthew 18:20 (NLT) "For where two or three gather together as my followers, I am there among them." That is God's promise and He never reneges on a promise. The workplace will be a better place with praying employees.

Know Your Company Surroundings

Respect the workplace and company policies concerning any type of religious boundaries. Know the company policies and adhere to them. It shows respect as well as integrity. If you are not allowed to have prayer publicly during the work hours, then maybe find a time when you are off work before or after the workday.

Gain permission from the authority and personal permission from the person you are praying for. Ask them if it would be OK to pray for them or their circumstances. Getting turned down from anyone you ask to pray for is a rarity. There have been two times out of thousands of interactions that someone said they did not want to pray with me or have me pray for them.

First and foremost, you are honoring God with your actions, then you are showing respect for the company and the people that you work close to daily. Primarily, you do this because you care for the people you work with and the company you work for.

Honor God

In everything you do, honor God, and show your love for people. Care about the lives of others. How do you honor God? Be kind, pleasant, approachable, and full of the Spirit.

You are His child, and He is your heavenly Father, your Creator, He always deserves the honor. That is who you are in Christ Jesus. Show Him in all your workplace situations.

How to Strengthen Prayer

You strengthen your prayer life by practicing. Just as a major league baseball pitcher that throws thousands of pitches over the plate just to stay in the game - The practice of prayer is especially important to development and consistency of a mature spiritual walk with your God.

Begin the day with a time of Prayer. Pray during the day as the Lord leads and circumstances and people will come your way.

Let your prayer be one of Thanksgiving before asking for anything. Be thankful to God for what you have already, your spouse, family home, work, etc...

Take time to be quiet before the Lord. Be still and know that He is God, and you are not. The biggest challenge whenever you begin is to make it happen consistently. Consistency will lead to a lifestyle of prayer and a stronger relationship with God.

When you become strong with this tool, you will experience a peace about everything that comes your way. You will have a clear discerning spirit that will be noticeable to others and you will be able to help others through tough circumstances.

As you learn to pray unceasingly, you will do mighty works with God.

PART THREE
THE RESULTS OF FAITH

CHAPTER ELEVEN

SERVING FROM THE HEART

Christian leadership happens as you bring your full self and all the tools to the table each day.

Leading with a Servant Heart

Jesus clearly explains to His disciples that the road of Spiritual greatness comes through servanthood. Matthew 23: 10-12 (NAS) "Do not be called leaders; for One is your Leader, *that is,* Christ." "But the greatest among you shall be your servant." "Whoever exalts himself shall be humbled; and whoever humbles himself shall be exalted." Mark 10:45 (NLT) "For even the Son of Man came not to be served but to serve others and to give his life as a ransom for many."

What does it mean to be a Christian leader? The Toner definition is a humble, kind, generously gracious influencer with the intention to serve others.

What leaders are not is described in Proverbs 8:13 (NLT) "All who fear the LORD will hate evil. Therefore, I hate pride and arrogance, corruption, and perverse speech." Most workers can remember the name of the worst leader they ever worked for. People leave companies because of the leaders that fail to lead. There are many examples of bad leadership. Each situation is different, but the common denominator is a leader that does not consider the people in the organization as valuable outside the profit they can generate. I served as a chaplain at a company that had a business owner who people were afraid to be around. The employees seemed to walk on eggshells when he was around. He watched everything they did, more of a micromanager than a trusting leader. The employees felt as if he did not care one bit about the people, he was responsible to lead.

The sad part about this owner was that he had me as the chaplain in the company, yet he did not live out his faith in his business. He was a professed Christian who was giving a bad name to Christianity. If you were looking for an example of a Christian leader, you would not want anything to do with his faith. That, in turn, reflected in his employees' trust in me as a pastor. I had several conversations with the owner about the atmosphere in the company. It seemed to go in one ear and out the other. People were coming and going at this company. He had a hard time retaining employees. No wonder why, leadership failed them.

What Does a Christian Leader Look Like?

Christian leaders are game changers in life. They will always seek God's directions so that others will see Christ in them. There are plenty of good Christian leaders in every industry in the workforce. These are people who put God first and show genuine care for the people that work in the companies they lead. As a Chaplain, I experienced only a handful of bad business owners. They were the exception. Most of the companies I served were led by good to great leaders. I could write a book on many good leaders that I have had the privilege to serve alongside. I learned so very much about leadership from these owners. I praise God for all the caring leaders who showed their employees just how valuable they were. Even if you do not own the company, act like you do. Own the actions, own your responsibilities, think like an owner.

I'll give you one example. When I served as a Chaplain in a medium size car dealership several years ago, I had the privilege of getting to know the owner of the business very well. This man had an intimidating physical presence about him that initially would put people on alert. You may have met people like that; the kind of person who stood out in a room. From the outside, he was an attractive man who smiled all the time. Not the kind of smile where you would question if he were up to something devious. He had a smile that invited conversation. He was a confident man who exuded a pleasant personality to everyone he met.

He welcomed me as his Chaplain right away. I felt comfortable from day one. The more I got to know this man, the more I could see how God was leading His life. He would have the door to his office open almost all the time so anyone could come in and speak with him. His desire was that each employee understand who God was and how God loved each of them. When someone had some troubles, he would immediately invite them to talk about their issues with either himself or me as their Chaplain. I was an extension of his work values in the company. He valued people as the most important asset. He treated everyone with respect and care. They saw Jesus in him very clearly. He had the Bible on his desk and studied it daily. It was his way of life. This leader was a servant to others without question. Do I have to tell you that he had a vibrant car dealership that people stayed with for years? He was a successful man at home and in business.

Interacting with Family

If you could investigate the home life of a Christian leader, you would see someone who thought before they spoke, who cared about those who lived in the house, and desired to make a home full of love for the family. Kindness would be the word that would describe their disposition. You could ask their spouse and they would say the same thing. They would be one of tenderness and compassion, always wanting the best for each family member.

Interacting with Community

A Christian leader is open for anything that would build people up. They are builders and influencers in the community. People look to them for direction and welcome any constructive feedback they share for the betterment of the folks in the neighborhood.

Results

The results you see a Christian leader produce can be calculated. They are considerably valuable with the maximum amount of involvement with the team. They value the people they work with and seek to achieve a common, significant outcome.

Reputation

The reputation of a Christian leader has lasting implications. They should be respectful, respected, and true to their word. Integrity is the groundwork of decisions and influence. Not religious, but relational. Not critical, but careful not to insult. Not hard, but soft hearted.

Leadership God's Way

Leading others begins with leading yourself. Matthew 7:12 (NLT) "Do to others whatever you would like them to do to you. This is the essence of all that is taught in the law and the prophets."

In a book by Henry and Richard Blackaby named "Spiritual Leadership" Broadman and Holman Publishers, 2001, Pg. 31, they mention that "as a leader grows personally, they increase their capacity to lead. As they increase their capacity to lead, they enlarge the capacity of their organization to grow." Richard says that the best thing they can do for an organization is to grow personally.

The question has come up many times if leaders are born or made. That is a good question that I can only speak about from experience. There are plenty of books written on the subject, but this is my book to you, so you are getting my life's experiences, not the academic version of leadership. The experiences that you have as a leader were most likely learned from the actions of others. You either adopted the characteristics from someone you learned from or you chose not to use what you saw or experienced. The characteristics of a leader are fashioned, understood, and practiced. A good leader will see the value in other people that lead and develop what works to influence those they interact with at work, home, or a social environment. You are going to lead based on who is leading you, in most cases. For a Christian leader, Jesus Christ must be your example.

First, lead yourself. It starts with you. You must have values, values in every aspect of your life. Where do you get these values? As a Christian leader your values must be grounded in the scriptures. God has outlined His values for you to follow. They must be yours as part of who you are. You should have a good understanding of how God sees you. Relying on how others see you as a leader can be important, but others must see how your actions on the outside match the heart you have on the inside. Your heart will show in your leadership towards others, whether you know it or not.

Take care of your home (internally). Just like an athlete, you train, strengthen and exercise. You practice staying in shape. Leadership needs maintenance, self-evaluation, and feedback. Pay close attention to your heart while practicing and getting feedback from people who see your works. Your faith will exude your works.

Guard and guide your heart. Proverbs 4:23 (NLT) says, "Guard your heart above all else, for it determines the course of your life." As a leader you must be aware of how the world can rob your intention. Stay in the Word of God and surround yourself with people who will strengthen you.

Scripture tells us about leadership principles. You can use these principles from scripture to fuel your leadership, especially within yourself.

Self-Leadership Principle #1

Philippians 2:4 (NAS) "do not merely look out for your own personal interests, but also for the interests of others."

Your focus should be outward only after you have self-evaluated inwardly. This is the gospel. Jesus came with redemption in mind. His thoughts were to bring His creation back to Him.

As a leader, we have the eyes and ears of others. We are being watched in all circumstances. Our testimony of who we are in Christ can change a life for our Lord. Just yield and listen to God's leading because there are no accidents with Him. We will have the opportunity to show His love for others each day, through our leadership.

Self-Leadership Principle #2

2 Tim 2:15 (NAS) "Be diligent to present yourself approved to God as a workman who does not need to be ashamed, accurately handling the word of truth."

A Spiritual leader must be true to God's Word. Being diligent in study will enhance leadership skills and prove to develop other leaders. You will see the fruit of your labor. God's character is true, efficient, and trustworthy. How you lead will give God the glory for developing a servant's heart towards others. It starts with your actions according to His Word.

This is a constant in your walk with our Lord. What you are learning about God will be evident in your daily interactions.

Self-Leadership Principle #3

Galatians 6:9 (ESV) "And let us not grow weary of doing good, for in due season we will reap, if we do not give up."

Being a leader will be tiresome, hard work and frustrating at times, but we should stay strong and never give up. God will lead you for you to influence others for Him. He will never leave you. He is your fortress, your strong tower, your everlasting Father.

This needs to start with you. It starts with God, but you take the responsibility to give over your will to learn, grow and practice what you learn from the Word. Get some rest, if the Lord does not come back tomorrow, you will have more work to do here on Earth.

CHAPTER TWELVE
THE HEARTBEAT OF A
CHRISTIAN LEADER AT WORK

What does it mean to focus on Christian leadership in the workplace? I met a man named Ed Silvoso several years ago at a leadership conference. Ed wrote a detailed book named **Anointed for Business**, *published by Regal books, 2002.* Ed's introduction is just as appropriate today as it was eighteen years ago when he wrote the book. He said "The marketplace – a synthesis of business, education and government – is to a metropolis what a heart is to the human body. Yet millions of men and women who have been called to ministry in the marketplace feel like second-class citizens when compared to those that serve in a church or missionary context. And they often fail to rise to their God-appointed position."

Ed's premise is that, as a believer in Jesus Christ, we have a responsibility and a duty to be a light in the place that we spend most of our time. We know from previous chapters that God is all-powerful, all-knowing, and everywhere, so there are no accidents with Him. He calls us to be a powerful witness in the place we interact with people the most, our workplace.

Ed points out that the last revival, the one prophesied by Joel and quoted by Peter in Acts 2:17-21, will take place all over the city and not just inside the church building. This is a powerful part of scripture that needs further study. I believe that the church building will not be where the people of God will flourish and contribute to God's kingdom with His people. I believe that the workplace will be a vital link that God will use to reach people and bring them to know His love and care and saving grace.

At least seven out of ten people in the workplace do not have a church home as we know it to be. They do not leave their houses on a particular morning (Sunday) to go to a place to be with other proclaimed believers. The place to reach people for Jesus is the workplace. We do that not by hitting people over the head with a "big fat Bible" (as my friend Mark Cress, Founder of Corporate Chaplains of America, would say), but by loving them into the kingdom of God. We are to lead people with our testimony in word and deed. We have a responsibility to share the love of Jesus wherever we go. We must know the Word of God or we will be no different than the folks who live a life without Christ in their own flesh.

The people of God are called to serve and lead as disciples. If you are a Christian and have a job or own a business, God expects you to show the love that He shows you to those you work alongside.

A Christian in the workplace is different in several ways.

Differentiator 1 – **Know the Word of God.** Focus on people development, God's gifting, and highlighting strengths. It is especially important for a Christian leader to know what God says in the Bible about how to lead. If we lead by example, we should have godly examples. We experience many different types of leaders inside and outside our place of work. Leaders need to know God has intimately called them into a position of influence in the company they serve. It is a divine appointment led by the King of Kings and the Lord of Lords.

Differentiator 2 – **Develop a Specific Vision** for people and the company. They are progressive in nature and know that the future is about the people they lead and the revenue they share. We will not be at a company forever and a business will not be in business forever. A company with a forward thinker that is kingdom focused will develop people to be independent, while thinking of others as more important than themselves. God must be glorified in the operation of the company.

Differentiator 3 – **Possess a Servant Attitude.** This characteristic of a Christian leader is most important. Jesus very clearly said that He came to serve and not to be served, if those words came from the leader, they should be emulated. A Christian leader is all about serving the interests of the people and the interests of the company with excellence. To serve others will bring about fruit in every aspect of personal development and company growth. Mark 10:45 (NLT) "For even the Son of Man came not to be served but to serve others and to give his life as a ransom for many."

A Christian leader in the workplace sets specific goals.

Goal 1 – **Embrace** your calling in the place you work. You have a purpose for working where you work. There is a plan that God has for you. Open your heart and know that God will direct your path. Get ready for the future.

Goal 2 – **Improve** your working environment. Excellence should be your word for the day, every day. Show that you are a reliable leader, that will show as an example for others to follow. Set your mind on constant improvement of the people you lead and the company you oversee.

Goal 3 – **Share** Jesus by your actions and words. The words and actions of a Christian leader should show clearly in everyday operations. Co-workers should notice a remarkable attitude that is pleasant, kind, inquisitive and results oriented.

How Christians Lead

Let us highlight 7 Foundations of Christian Leadership in the Workplace:

Leadership Foundation #1 – **A Servants Heart**

> *Matthew 20:26 (NLT) "But among you it will be different. Whoever wants to be a leader among you must be your servant,"*

This calls you to be servant minded. Think of ways you can serve your people better. Make serving others part of your DNA. Service is sacrifice at times, but always faithful and fruitful.

Jesus came to serve. His character was always focused on others. We are to be like Christ in our attitudes to serve those we work alongside.

Simply look out for the needs of others at the same time you notice how the operation of the business is being handled. Listen to the concerns of the people you lead, then act on their concerns. Actions always speak louder than words.

Leadership Foundation #2 – **Work Hard**

> *2 Timothy 2:15 (NLT) "Work hard so you can present yourself to God and receive his approval. Be a good worker, one who does not need to be ashamed and who correctly explains the word of truth."*

Show the people you work with that you would not expect them to do what you are not willing to do yourself. Be an example for others to follow.

God is a God of excellence and sacrifice. How you handle the people you lead and the resources you have will tell a story about your integrity that God expects and shows you.

The workplace is a place that needs solid Christian leadership. Companies' welcome leaders who will do the right thing all the time and set an example so others will see the good works and desire to develop for a bright future.

Leadership Foundation #3 – **Be Unselfish**

> *Philippians 2:3 (NLT) "Don't be selfish; don't try to impress others. Be humble, thinking of others as better than yourselves."*

Allow the people you lead to see your godly attitude. They should see humility and an obvious desire to see others grow personally, focusing on others always. God sent His Son for us, so that by the gift of Jesus, we can show God's love to others.

Be gracious in your praise for others as they stand out. Be a giver of time and resources.

Leadership Foundation #4 – **Stand Strong**

Isaiah 41:10 (NLT) "Don't be afraid, for I am with you. Do not be discouraged, for I am your God. I will strengthen you and help you. I will hold you up with my victorious right hand."

There will be times when you are just worn out physically, mentally, and spiritually. Rest and get back in the work of your Lord.

This calls you to understand that there will be tough times ahead. A great example is what is happening as I write this book. A virus has infiltrated the world and it has people in great fear for their lives. God knows exactly what is happening and he desires for people to come closer to Him during times like this. He promises to strengthen and give us hope. He is our strength. He is always faithful and shows His power in overcoming fear. Trust in Him during troubled times.

As a leader, people are watching how you deal with troubling situations. Your faith will be obvious when trials come in your workplace or your personal life. You can lead through tough times with God's help, impacting others for your Lord.

Leadership Foundation #5 – **Find a Solid Mentor**

Hebrews 13:7 (NLT) "Remember your leaders who taught you the word of God. Think of all the good that has come from their lives and follow the example of their faith."

Have a person that you can rely on hold you accountable for your actions and leadership, usually someone you respect that knows the Word of God and has shown you what leadership looks like in another person. God has touched other leaders that have passed on His characteristics - so that you can do the same.

Perpetuate what you have learned from your leaders. You will have an impact on others as you were impacted. Encourage others to find someone that can hold them accountable. Possibly establish a mentor program within the company.

Leadership Foundation #6 – **Good Works are Godly Evidence**

Galatians 6:9 (NAS) "Let us not lose heart in doing good, for in due time we will reap if we do not grow weary."

Continue to work out your faith with goodness. People will see your good works and your Father in heaven will be glorified. God is good all the time, there is nothing bad in Him. His character in you is evidence of His goodness, you will see the results in other people.

Show your strength by doing good towards the people at work. Do not give up on them.

Leadership Foundation #7 – **Share Jesus**

John 3:16 (ESV) "For God so loved the world, that He gave His only Son, that whoever believes in Him should not perish but have eternal life."

Share your faith with others as God opens a door. Do not force the door. Allow Him to open an opportunity. Ask permission to share your heart with others as you lead.

God's character will show through you. He is the hope of the world. Share Hope. Share His character.

As mentioned earlier some workplaces have boundaries for sharing your faith as a leader. Be aware of the boundaries and do it right. Show integrity while showing love to co-workers or the folks you lead. Build trust so that you will be welcomed to share what God is doing in your life. It is a matter of life and death.

CONCLUSION: WORK FOR GOD - WORK FOR EXCELLENCE - BE THE INFLUENCER

This book is a call to Servant Leadership, right where you are. Our Christian walk is especially important in such volatile times in our nation's history. The personal life challenges we experience affect every aspect of our being. Our home and the place we work are where we spend most of our time. What we have done all the way up to this very moment will define who we are and how we have affected the lives of others. We all have a story that will touch people in different ways. The hope of this book is for you as the reader to empathize with some of the experiences. Learn from some of your troubles and tell them to other people. Maybe it is a book or even a simple kind gesture that will change an attitude. The amazement comes when you share what God has done in you that changes the lives of others forever.

There are no accidents with God. He is Omnipotent (all powerful), Omniscient (all knowing), Omnipresent (everywhere). He knows what you have gone through and who you interacted with through your life so far. The personal relationships you have developed are vital. You have touched others with your life, and they have touched you with theirs. Never take any of the experiences you have had for granted.

The stories in this book were real life testimonies not unlike what other people go through. The biggest difference is how we all deal with the folks we meet from the perspective of our unique experiences.

Life is precious, from day one until the end. This is not Fantasy Island, but real heart changing events that happen every day all around the world to people like you and me. Giving someone hope in a time of depression or praying for someone that loses a loved one, your life becomes valuable to someone else. The better we take care of this life, the stronger our influence will be on the folks we see each day at home, work, or the church you attend.

Hearts at Work is your journey, from the memories of childhood through the times of challenging experiences. Hearts at Work is active each day in how you lead your family. The work of your heart is evident through the influences you have at your workplace.

You were created to experience unique challenges of all kinds. God pushed you through every time, sometimes pulling you through your own stubbornness. So, here you are. Now what? Gather your thoughts, experiences, heart changes, depressive times, healed pains, and spiritual evaluations, and give them away to other people. You have experience now. What will you do with those experiences? Experiences can be for other people to hear and learn from. Give your heart away on purpose this very day. Tell your heart story, that is what **Hearts at Work** is all about.

CHAPTER REFLECTIONS AND INSIGHT

A Closer Look Inside Our Personal "Heart at Work"

Chapter 1 – Attack of the Heart

1. What areas in your life do you spend the most time on? Family, Work, or The Lord?

2. What would a friend say to you about your relationship with the Lord? What fruits would they see concerning your priorities?

3. Spiritually, where are you? Write down three things that you are willing to change today.

Chapter 2 – Forgiveness of the Heart

1. What is the first thing that must happen within you before you can forgive anyone? What does the Bible say about forgiveness?

2. When someone hurt you in the past, how did you forgive them, and do they know you forgave them? Is there someone who has hurt you that you need to forgive?

3. If you are married, when was the last time you said "I'm sorry" to your spouse and how did they respond? What would you tell someone who has a hard time forgiving their spouse or another person?

Chapter 3 – Healing of the Heart

1. Who is someone right now that you need to forgive for hurting you with words or actions?

2. What experience have you had in the past with forgiveness – whether good or bad?

3. Beginning with your relationship with God, what does it mean to you when Jesus says, "Father, forgive them for they do not know what they are doing?"

Chapter 4 – Depression of the Heart

1. What are some ways that people are broken? What does restoration look like?

2. What are three things you could do or say to someone who is depressed?

3. If you had someone tell you they wanted to end their lives, what would you say to them? What are a few of the steps you would take to make sure that would not happen?

Chapter 5 – Spirit of the Heart

1. What would you have said if Pete asked you what to do with his wife's concerns about him going to church?

2. Tell of a time when you could have or should have told someone about Jesus but did not. You had the chance, and you blew it.

3. What area of personal growth needs more attention? How do you intend to strengthen your walk with your Lord?

4. You had the chance, and you blew it. Tell of a time when you could or should have told someone about Jesus but did not.

    a. Having read this chapter, what do you feel you could do differently to prepare you for the next opportunity

Chapter 6 – Reflections of the Heart

1. What are some of the differences in the way God sees you and how you see yourself?

2. From God's perspective, what ways can you show His love outside your home to others?

3. What could your godly perspective do to help others grow? Name three areas.

Chapter 7 – God of the Heart

1. What is it about the place you work that you would like to see changed for the better? What are the names of some people who you would love to see come to a personal relationship with the Lord? Pray for them!

2. What are some practical ways you could share your faith with people at work?

3. What question or questions might you ask a co-worker that would begin a spiritual conversation?

Chapter 8 – Spiritual Practice of the Heart

1. If you were in front of a judge and he asked for evidence of God's Spirit working in you, what evidence would you present? What would people say was different about you and the way you conduct yourself?

2. What does it mean for you to be holy?

3. What are some ways God has sustained you over your lifetime when you deserved bad results, but He showed mercy?

Chapter 9 – Gods' Love Letter to the Heart

1. What would be a good time each day that you could read your Bible? What version do you own?

2. What are the names of three people you know that could help you with a Bible study? Call them and ask them to hold you accountable for reading the Word.

3. What do you know about the Bible? What are a couple of ways you could live out your faith in the workplace?

4. What are a couple of ways you could live out your faith in the workplace?

Chapter 10 – Praying from the Heart

1. Name two things you took away from this chapter on prayer.

2. What are the names of two people right now who you work with that need prayer? Pray for them NOW!

3. When would be the best time for you to be quiet before the Lord on a consistent basis? Schedule that NOW.

Chapter 11 – Serving from the Heart

1. Based on what you read, how would you define personal leadership?

2. Explain a situation where you experienced bad leadership? Good leadership?

3. Name a scripture that would explain a characteristic of a good leader? Google it, if you need to. Search: Bible verse on Christian leadership.

Chapter 12 – The Heartbeat of a Christian leader at Work

1. Leadership starts with you. What are three characteristics of a good leader?

2. What are two characteristics of a servant leader?

3. Identify two strong points and two areas that need work in your personal leadership style.